THE GOSPEL IS
REST

The Gospel is Rest: Secrets of the Divine Covenant of Peace

Copyright © 2023 Jacklyn Paletta

Scriptures taken from the Holy Bible, New International Version®, NIV®. Copyright © 1973, 1978, 1984, 2011 by Biblica, Inc.™ Used by permission of Zondervan. All rights reserved worldwide. www.zondervan.com The "NIV" and "New International Version" are trademarks registered in the United States Patent and Trademark Office by Biblica, Inc.™ | Scripture quotations marked "Phillips" are taken from The New Testament in Modern English, copyright 1958, 1959, 1960 J.B. Phillips and 1947, 1952, 1955, 1957 The Macmillian Company, New York. Used by permission. All rights reserved. | All Scripture quotations marked MSG taken from THE MESSAGE, copyright © 1993, 2002, 2018 by Eugene H. Peterson. Used by permission of NavPress, represented by Tyndale House Publishers. All rights reserved., | Scripture quotations taken from the Amplified® Bible (AMP), Copyright © 2015 by The Lockman Foundation. Used by permission. www.lockman.org. | Scripture quotations marked TPT are from The Passion Translation®. Copyright © 2017, 2018 by Passion & Fire Ministries, Inc. Used by permission. All rights reserved. ThePassionTranslation.com. | Scripture quotations taken from the (NASB®) New American Standard Bible®, Copyright © 1960, 1971, 1977, 1995, 2020 by The Lockman Foundation. Used by permission. All rights reserved. www.lockman.org. | Scripture taken from the New King James Version®. Copyright © 1982 by Thomas Nelson. Used by permission. All rights reserved. | The Holy Bible, English Standard Version® (ESV®) Copyright © 2001 by Crossway, a publishing ministry of Good News Publishers. All rights reserved. ESV Text Edition: 2016. | Scripture quotations marked (NLT) are taken from the Holy Bible, New Living Translation, copyright ©1996, 2004, 2015 by Tyndale House Foundation. Used by permission of Tyndale House Publishers, Carol Stream, Illinois 60188. All rights reserved.

This book is set in the typeface *Athelas* designed by Veronika Burian and Jose Scaglione.

Paperback ISBN: 978-1-955546-42-3

A Publication of *Tall Pine Books*
119 E Center Street, Suite B4A | Warsaw, Indiana 46580
www.tallpinebooks.com

| 1 23 23 20 16 02 |

Published in the United States of America

THE GOSPEL IS
REST

SECRETS *of* THE DIVINE
COVENANT *of* PEACE

JACKLYN PALETTA

"Jacklyn's book *The Gospel is Rest* is a life changer. Her personal moments intertwined with Holy Spirit God moments literally open your heart to what God is saying to you. It is a deeply needed perspective shift for doing life in a world full of extreme highs and rugged lows. It is one of those books you want to read slowly as you meditate on the powerful scripture applications and let the prophetic insights burrow deep in your heart and mind. As a mother, a pastor, a widow, a friend, there is a wealth of biblical study and application that is so rich and so deep, I can't wait to use it for Life Group study. The activation steps at the end of each chapter really help the reader to stop and apply healthy adjustments to our lives. This book draws you in, wraps your soul in God's invitation to dwell in peace and leaves you still lingering on the heart changes God can do on any day, no matter the circumstances you face."

—REV. JENNIFER PASQUALE
President *International Christian Fellowship Churches of Italy*
Lead Pastor *International Christian Fellowship Rome*
Thankful Mother of Jacklyn Paletta

"I love it when truth impacts my thinking. Jacklyn tackles the ever chasing thing we call *rest,* and might I add...nails it. So little, good thought is written today about this critical need. I love the covenant theme about rest she reveals in her book. She just might help you change your thinking. You know what they say, "Change your thinking, change your life." Enjoy!"

—RON HEITMAN
Lead Pastor of *Evangel Church*

"From the beginning to the end of *The Gospel is Rest*, Jacklyn Paletta does a fantastic job outlining in detail what the Word of God tells us about finding and abiding in the peace and presence of the Lord. In ministry it's often seen as a weakness to get away and rest, even though Jesus modeled this for us.

I love this statement by Jacklyn... "You can't change what you won't acknowledge." As leaders and believers until we acknowledge our need for Biblical rest we will keep burning the candle at both ends until we are completely burned out."

—ANDY PARKS
Lead Pastor of *Cross Point Church*

"*The Gospel is Rest* is a life giving perspective that will change how we think, talk, live, love, serve, and apply scripture to our everyday lives. Jacklyn takes us on a journey to discover the beauty of rest and the strength that comes from rest. The transformation that happens when we begin reading the Gospel through the lens of rest leads to freedom. *The Gospel is Rest* is not a workbook we work through but a book that works in us and through us.

—CAROLINE DUNN
Founder of *Reach One Europe*

"This book's message is one of profound wisdom: "Abiding in rest is not the absence of restlessness. It is not an event but a development of intimacy that takes a lifetime as a believer!" I believe that Jacklyn's message of learning to live from a place of rest will be one that will transform our everyday life - whether seasoned or a new believer in Christ; I encourage you to do a reflective intake of how you can connect to the gospel of rest."

—Pastor Laura Lee
Stateside Partner Development Director
for *Inspire Global Sisterhood*

"A beautifully balanced look at the truth of scripture and how this peace can overflow into our day-to-day lives. This book is desperately needed in our noisy, media saturated society. I know it will help believers everywhere enter into the promise of restful worship."

—Daniel J. Henderson
Media Messengers

"*The Gospel is Rest* is a tremendous, awe-inspiring book that unleashes the capacity for your mind to operate from the position of rest that God intended. From Jacklyn's experiences to her in-depth look at what the scripture speaks about rest, you will find yourself uplifted, educated and self-reflective. Each chapter challenges you to ask yourself deep questions and helps to facilitate change in your mindsets. I highly recommend this book to everyone. It will be deeply beneficial for prayer groups, small groups, spouses and families to read together."

—Amy Henderson
Homeschool Mother of 5

"From the beginning of this book I instantly connected with the theme of finding rest in Jesus. I think this topic resonates with everyone in today's society. Even if we are not busy we think the cool thing is to say "I'm busy". Jacklyn's personal stories weaved throughout will have you remembering moments in your life of God's faithfulness. Finding rest has stuck with me since I started reading and look forward to hearing the lives it impacts. Also Jacklyn's sincere heart and love for Jesus jumps off the pages and you can discern her personality throughout the book. Allow God to speak to you through this book and find Rest!"

—BO GERKEN
Lead Pastor of *Living Proof Church*

"*The Gospel is Rest* is a timely read for anyone exhausted by constantly looking for peace. This book shares what true rest, lasting peace, looks like. Jacklyn authentically shares examples from her life that have been anything but peaceful. However, through those circumstances, she has come to experience firsthand what it means to live from a place of rest, which is available to all believers. She beautifully points the reader to biblical truth, challenging them to not just read the words that she has written but THE WORD. At the end of each chapter, there is an activation section to encourage practicing the principles within its pages. These add to the spiritual impact this book will undoubtedly have on each person who reads it."

—HEIDI L. ROBIDOU
Coordinator *WOVEN Women's Ministries*
AGK Ministry Network

CONTENTS

Foreword I

Preface 3

PART ONE: WHAT IS BIBLICAL REST?

1. My Journey.. 13
2. What is Rest?..27
3. Case Studies on Rest 41

PART TWO: HOW CAN WE REST?

4. Be Still and Know.................................... 75
5. Know God 95
6. Know Yourself.. 113
7. Learn to Abide 125
8. Rest in Action 149

PART THREE: WHY CAN WE REST?

9. Holy Spirit...163
10. God is My Source 171
11. The Mind of Christ 189
12. Kingdom Authority...............................205

Conclusion 217
About the Author....................................221
Also By...223
Endnotes 225

FOREWORD

IT HAS BEEN an absolute joy to know Jacklyn for nearly three decades. From a young girl ministering alongside her family to becoming an author, a lawyer, and a mother, I have witnessed Jacklyn always living life with the perfect balance of grace and tenacity. I have seen Jacklyn overcome some of life's toughest challenges and, though she had every right to grow bitter and hard-hearted, she only grew more compassionate and more in love with her Savior. Jacklyn is nothing short of an inspiration, and the way that she shines the love of Jesus on everything she does draws in anyone who meets her.

It is no wonder that the same inspiration and light radiate throughout this entire book. On every page, Jacklyn's vulnerability easily allows readers to relate to the stress and overwhelming scenarios life forces us all into, regardless of age, social status, or spiritual maturity. Yet at the end of every chapter, Jacklyn invites readers to sit in the warm embrace of a God who desires to give His children rest.

Like Jacklyn, I have faced many days where rest seemed a near impossible find. However, after only the second chapter, I found myself reminded that rest is not something we have to find because Christ has already created a path to it. What we must do, as Jacklyn points out, is enter into the covenant of peace that Christ has offered us and operate every day from the rest for which He has made us.

I invite you to take this book to heart and I pray that God will truly allow the words, exercises, and journal prompts to present the gospel in a way you may have never thought of it before: a gospel of rest.

—GAIL CLAY
Christ Follower, Mother, *and* Mimi

PREFACE

WHAT IF YOU could work, parent, minister, friend from a place of rest instead of toward a place of rest?

What if you didn't have to work for the weekend because the "weekend" is a place you're working from?

What if you didn't have to plan, save, pack, and travel to take that vacation for a much needed mental break because you learned how to work from a place of rest?

What if you could learn how to get quiet and be still while still navigating the activities of life?

Have you ever met a person who seemed to carry or exude peace? Wherever they went, they just seemed to have a calm about them? Have you ever had a season where you felt that way about yourself or people in your life expressed that sentiment about you? What if you could live there? What if you were so "rested" that your default position was peace and not stress?

Charles H. Spurgeon said, "No tongue can tell the depth of that calm which comes over the soul which has received the peace of God which passeth all understanding." It is this peace, this abiding rest, that we explore in the chapters that follow.

In this book, we will examine the biblical prescription for rest and how God not only invites us to rest, He provides while we are resting. Before you finish reading these pages, you will know how to implement practical tools so that you can abide in a place of rest.

My prayer for you and theme for this journey can be found in Ephesians 3:16-19 (AMP) and Psalm 27:1 (AMP):

> *"May He grant you out of the riches of His glory, to be **strengthened and spiritually energized** <u>with</u> **power through His Spirit** in your inner self, [indwelling your innermost being and **personality**], so that Christ may dwell in your hearts through your faith. And may you, having been [**deeply**] **rooted and** [**securely**] **grounded in** love, be fully capable of comprehending with all the saints (God's people) the width and length and height and depth of His love [**fully experiencing that amazing, endless love**]; and [that you may come] to know [practically, through personal experience] the love of Christ which far surpasses [mere] knowledge [without experience], that you may be **filled up** [**throughout your being**] **to all the fullness of God** [so that you may have the richest experience of God's presence in your lives, completely filled and flooded with **God Himself.**]"* (Ephesians 3:16-19 AMP)

There's a lot to unpack in those verses, but basically there are four things in these verses I believe are key to abiding in *REST*:

1. Be strengthened and spiritually energized;
2. Be rooted and grounded in love;
3. Experience that amazing, endless love;
4. Be filled up with all the fullness of God.

In the following pages, we will explore how these four keys are established in our lives through the covenant of rest. (Spoiler alert: It starts with the Holy Spirit.)

Psalm 27:1 is a little more concise: *"The Lord is the refuge and fortress of my life."* Here the point is that we do not provide our sanctuary, solitude, constitution, and fortitude. If we rest in the character and nature of God Himself, IN Him we will find our refuge and fortress.

THE GOSPEL IS REST

The word *gospel* is derived from the Anglo-Saxon term *godspell*, meaning "good story," a rendering of the Latin *evangelium* and the Greek *evangelion*, meaning "good news" or "good telling."

The origination of the title for this book flows from the literal translation of the word *gospel* and the realization that the kingdom realm is here. The "good news" is that all the attributes we imagine are involved with eternal rest do not have to await an eschatological initiation sequence. (You don't have to wait until you die to have peace.) Instead, when we abide in Christ, when we dwell in the secret place, when we abide under the shadow of the Almighty and allow the Lord to be our refuge and fortress, we partner with His identity (see Psalm 91 and Psalm 27:1) and live from His oasis of rest.

If there was a worship song that would help me convey the essence of the message, it would be "Firm Foundation" by Austin Davis, Chandler Moore, and Cody Carnes.

The first verse contains the lyrics:

> *When everything around me is shaken I've never been more glad*
> *That I put my faith in Jesus 'Cause He's never let me down*

The message conveys the heart of the *Gospel is Rest*. We can exude peace, even when the situation may warrant different characteristics. In verse two, they take it a bit deeper:

> *I've still got joy in chaos*
> *I've got peace that makes no sense I won't be going under*
> *I'm not held by my own strength 'Cause I've built my life on Jesus*

He never asked us to do anything in our own strength. We're going to make it through all that comes our way because our own strength does not hold us. He undergirds us, fights for us,

"IF WE REST IN THE CHARACTER AND NATURE OF GOD HIMSELF, IN HIM WE WILL FIND OUR REFUGE AND FORTRESS."

and enables us as we partner with Him. (Consider pausing for a moment to listen to that song to further prepare your heart as you investigate this good news. In the version released by Jenn Johnson, she invites the worshippers to pause to consider the heart of the message. I invite you to pull that up on your favorite streaming platform, and take a moment to re-calibrate before you continue reading.)

APPLYING THE PRINCIPLES

As we learn what it is to rest, we will engage in a process I will refer to as "activation." This is a process by which we will invite the Holy Spirit to search our hearts and minds and reveal supernatural truths to us. For some of us, this may be new or feel weird. The reality is in so doing, we allow the Holy Spirit to do His job:

> "But the Helper (Comforter, Advocate, Intercessor— Counselor, Strengthener, Standby), the Holy Spirit, whom the Father will send in My name [in My place, to represent Me and act on My behalf], **He will teach you all things. And He will help you remember everything that I have told you.**" (John 14:26 AMP)

This concept is echoed a couple chapters later:

> "But when He, the Spirit of Truth, comes, **He will guide you into all the truth** [full and complete truth]. For He will not speak on His own initiative, but He will speak whatever He hears [from the Father—the message regarding the Son], and He will disclose to you what is to come [in the future]." (John 16:13 AMP)

From a practical standpoint, activation looks like getting quiet. Listening. Holy Spirit enables and empowers us to hear from God, not dissimilar from how you may hear your own name should you think it in your mind. You can practice now. Close your eyes and in your mind say your own name. God speaks to us in much the same way. Sometimes, it's just a knowing.

For me, it seems to come more from my heart or stomach area than from my head. Still, I often sense His guidance with the same annunciation as my own thoughts. Sometimes hearing God comes as a thought or question. In the natural, we are selfish, confused, fretful, and chaotic. God is peace, clarity, and gentle, often revealing one small step at a time.

This assistance provided by the Holy Spirit is described in 1 Corinthians 2:

> *"But God now **unveils** these profound realities to us **by the Spirit**. Yes, he has **revealed** to us his inmost heart and deepest mysteries **through the Holy Spirit**, who constantly explores all things... And we articulate these realities with the words **imparted** to us **by the Spirit** and not with the words taught by human wisdom. **We join together Spirit-revealed truths with Spirit-revealed words."** (1 Corinthians 2:10, 13 TPT)

So, if it is unfamiliar to you, when you come to an activation at the end of a chapter, just relax. Take a slow cleansing breath. Lay all your worry, confusion, or fear at the feet of Jesus and allow the Holy Spirit to speak to you. It will get easier with each activation.

You will notice that I have recommended a praise or worship song to enhance the activation experience. Feel free to play the song on whatever streaming platform you choose. If you would rather not involve music, or you have a song or playlist to draw from, that's fine, too.

Open your heart as we journey into the secrets of the divine covenant of peace.

Holy Spirit, we invite You to unveil the truth about God's plan for divine rest. We ask You to uncover the ways in which we can lean into You more. We welcome You as You reveal the Father's heart toward us. We wait on You with anticipation. In Jesus' name, amen.

PART ONE

*"'Though the mountains be shaken and the hills be removed, yet my unfailing love for you will not be shaken **nor my covenant of peace be removed**,' says the Lord, who has compassion on you."* (Isaiah 54:10 NIV)

What exactly is rest? Is it an event? Is it a destination? Is it a thing we do while we're on vacation? In Part One, we will explore what rest means. We will discover what it looks like to rest, examine what the Bible says about rest, and learn that rest is an operating system. It is a way of being that Jesus Himself modeled.

If you find yourself striving or longing for an end to your restlessness, Part One may help you define what you're truly looking for.

CHAPTER 1

MY JOURNEY

MY JOURNEY TO learning how to abide in rest began in late April of 2020. My parents had been visiting from Italy. My mom came to stay with us in February for a few weeks to help me. My daughters had been extremely ill, were in and out of the hospital, and back and forth from multiple doctor appointments of varying specialties. And actually, looking back now, I realize I was operating from a restless perspective. My girls weren't miraculously healed overnight as I had wanted. God allowed us to go through a process of divine appointments and used doctors and medicine to bring some freedom to areas of health that had been troublesome.

By the time my mom arrived in February, we were five months into that process and had appropriate medicine and a plan for complete restoration, but I was weary. In those February moments of desperation, I couldn't see the proverbial forest for my trees were too big. Only now, in remembering, do I see things for what they really were.

At thirty-eight years old, I needed my mom. I just needed help, like Aaron and Hur kind of help. What I didn't know at the time was that God knew. God knew exactly what we would need and when we would need it. Because I was weary to the point of requesting my parents to send my mom, the path was set for my parents, who live in Italy, with its own epicenter for Covid-19, to be with us. Because my mom had already come, my father was also willing to come. Had my mother been in Italy, we are certain they would have stayed there, and waited out the pandemic. Because my father wanted to be with my mom, he was able to teach my daughters to ride a bike, build puzzles with them, have races, and make memories. Because he got here by early March, his travel-induced quarantine was over in time for them to go to California to be with my sister during the birth of her third child. And so, they left our home in the beginning of April.

In the preceding thirty days, we had stockpiled canned vegetables, toilet paper, bottled water, ammunition, medicine, medical supplies, and cleaning supplies. My husband had built a safe room in the basement, just in case people got too crazy because of the pandemic. We had panic drills with our children to prepare for the worst. By the time my parents left in the beginning of April, the restlessness I had from worrying about my daughters gave way to anxiousness rooted in fear, panic, and maybe even cabin fever.

You see, what we experienced were produce aisles without produce and butcher departments without meat. We resorted to shopping at Big Lots to acquire canned goods. Everything in our area was closed. Even the places like Home Depot, who were allowed to remain open for emergencies, had many aisles blocked off. We were not allowed to buy seeds or plants. We weren't even allowed to buy American flags.

In addition, our community was embroiled in racial conflict, resulting in looting, overturned police cars, and violence.

On April 28, 2020, our governor announced that we were finally allowed to go to our vacation or other homes if we chose. Well, our vacation home happened to be a Class C motorhome. That night, we packed that capsule like it was Armageddon. Every storage area was filled with supplies, canned food, clothes for every season, water, medicine, medical supplies, and various types of personal defense and hunting equipment. We truly didn't know when we would return. We left that night and didn't stop until we reached South Dakota's Badlands. We were in search of rest. We were looking for peace.

My husband and I both worked remotely because of the pandemic, I as an attorney and he as a financial advisor. The courts were closed and communication with clients and others easily occurred via phone, Zoom, or email. We did not tell our respective jobs that we were traveling. Instead, we Zoomed in or called in to all of our commitments at the appropriate times and handled business electronically. Since those obligations only occupied a small portion of a day, much time was spent being a family. We played games, fished, hiked, laughed, told stories, built fires, and had adventures. We realized that we had spent far too much time *doing* and not nearly enough time *being* a family. We explored South Dakota, Wyoming, every entrance of Yellowstone, Montana, Idaho, Utah, Colorado, Kansas, and more. It had always been my husband's dream to go on such a spontaneous adventure, but we were always too busy. I thought that "maybe someday when the kids were grown and we were retired, we could travel for weeks or months at a time, but in reality, my husband's goal was a pipe dream."

As days became weeks, we grew less inclined to return home. Whatever we had been doing at home was certainly not something we wanted to do ever again. This new rest, this new mode of operation, was what we wanted to become normal. At that point though, there was no way for us to cogently express the change that we were going to make, and certainly not with words that our families would understand. And so, we continued searching for rest, a resting place, or a refuge.

For a fleeting moment, my husband wondered if maybe that looked like a bunker. So, we went to an abandoned military outpost in southwestern South Dakota, in the middle of absolutely nowhere, that had earthen bunkers as far as the eye could see. Apparently, a doomsday prepper company had purchased this place and sold the bunkers to private citizens.

Okay, first of all, our daughters were five and six years old and our son was twelve. None of them are introverts. Friends, community, and the conveniences of a suburban modern lifestyle are important to all three of them. We are not independently wealthy. While we had saved money in our rainy-day fund, it would surely not cover more than several months of rainy days. Provision for our family was based on our employment. We thought we were looking for a destination, and if not a permanent place, at least one that would serve as an Alamo if needed. As much as there may be security in this place, it was not a viable option. So, we continued our search for a resting place.

I remembered that my company had offices in Kansas City. While we knew we would not want to live in such a city, we quickly learned that plenty of rural locations were within driving distance of the office. So, we decided there was no harm in looking there.

We contacted a realtor who asked for pictures of our current home and neighborhood because he anticipated we would just transplant to something similar. Finally, the day had come for our first meeting with him. As if we were the Griswolds on family vacation, we drove the RV to the business plex to meet the realtor.

Ultimately, he had us ride in his car to see the homes he had picked for us to visit. Each one was in a neighborhood not dissimilar from the one we were escaping back home. The thought of returning home to pack and move and relocate to one of these homes he was showing us became increasingly unsettling. Each home we visited, we lingered for fewer minutes than the one before it.

This was not what we were searching for.

Since we could not convey what we were looking for, the realtor gave us a link to all available listings. We started looking for homes which were situated on acreage. We would drive by them in the RV, and most were eliminated before bringing them to our realtor's attention. Finally, we narrowed it down to a manageable list we could visit with his help.

Ultimately, we found it!

We had the opportunity to meet the original owners of the home we were about to purchase. They graciously allowed us to keep our motorhome on their property before closing.

While standing in the driveway of our soon-to-be new home,

my husband reached out his hand to introduce himself. As he did, the owner reached out his hand and said, "Hi, I'm Moses." My husband paused and then stuttered in disbelief as he replied, "Hi, my name is Joshua." We pray for divine appointments; something happened in that exchange. It seemed to be the affirmation they both needed to know it was time for the baton to pass from Moses to Joshua. That encounter was revelatory confirmation that we were exactly where God wanted us.

We found the new house at the end of May, went home, and listed our own house for sale. The buyer made an offer the next day and all ensuing transactions were completed by July 31, 2020. When we found the house, it was unclear whether transferring within my company and keeping my job was an option. But we just *knew* we had to continue to move forward.

The meeting with my bosses went better than I could have imagined. They were supportive and excited about the opportunities for growth my move would have on the other office. AND I could still work from home as much as I wanted.

The confirmations continued.

Our new home was a working horse farm on over 11 acres, complete with barn, outbuildings, and chicken coop. The horses didn't stay, but the chickens did. Now, my husband and I are at least third generation suburbanites with zero farm experience, training, or education to speak of. After we got moved, we had no idea what to do next. It was as if we felt, "Okay, we got here. Now what?"

Our daughters were excited about the new adventure. In one of the first days there, our youngest exclaimed, "I'll go check for eggs!" as she ran toward the chicken coop. She had opened the door and walked into the coop when she started screaming bloody murder! Initially, I thought she had been stung by a bee or a wasp or something, which must have startled her. But then I could make out through her screams, "A snake! A snake!" as she was running toward us. So, I was just thinking, "Well, it must be a little garter snake or something. Suburbia meet farm life; things in rural America are all so unfamiliar, we will just have to get used to little snakes and things."

In the fifteen seconds it took for her to reach us, the same amount of time it took me to assure myself this is just part of adjusting to farm life, she had worked herself into not only screaming but also crying. This was very unusual for her. My heart dropped. "What kind of snake could bring my daughter to terror?"

As we all got closer to the coop and peered inside, we saw a baseball-width black snake curled multiple times around in a box where the chickens sit on their eggs. Before I could process everything, my husband had gotten his .22 rifle. He carefully put the barrel through the chicken wire screen and repeatedly shot this snake.

When we first spotted it, it was still, but curled around multiple times; now that it had been shot, more times than I could count, it was moving like crazy. My kids and I were on the deck before we realized we had moved from the coop.

Ultimately, my husband retrieved a rake and threw the snake out of the box and onto the grass. He doesn't even know how many times he shot the thing before it was all said and done.

He even used a shovel and chopped off its head, but it would not stop moving. The tape measure revealed that this big black snake was over six feet long!

Our adventure quickly turned to second guessing: What have we done? Where on earth did we just move our family? We have no idea how to deal with megalithic snakes! What other living surprises are in store for us if there are megalithic, terrorizing, black snakes? OH NO!

We still thought rest was a place, and we were suddenly concerned that maybe this place was not it.

Chaotic conversations in my mind soon gave way to reason. Just do the next right thing: unpack, put away, decorate, get ready for school to start. Not sure if there was an acceleration anointing on those tasks or if I just immersed myself in them so deeply, it was a "time flies when you're having fun" type thing. Either way, I ran out of "next right things to do" quicker than I anticipated.

Then it was, "Okay, we bought a farm. What *kind* of farm should we have?" Well, it seemed like the right thing to do to go to the livestock auction and see other people's animals from afar to assess whether any of those may be right for us.

So remember, I was born and raised in suburbia. I do not personally know one person who raises cattle. My experience was limited: a friend had a daughter in 4-H who showed us her cow. That kind of limited. So, dressed in my jeans, covered with tall black boots and my uncle's army jacket, we braved the auction.

If you've never been to a livestock auction, this one had wooden bleachers which formed a half circle around this pen on the floor of the arena. Three or so guys sat behind a table with a microphone and one navigated a computer. At the same time, another smashed all of his words together as if speaking a foreign language, calling out a whole bunch of numbers in a sequence unlike any you have ever heard. Three or so more guys were opening and closing doors and gates that led to the pen where they shuffled cows through as they were being bid on. Inside the pen were additional barricades or gates behind which grown men were hiding while wielding long handled plastic paddle type things.

I'm not sure what I thought a pet cow would potentially be like, but whatever it was, was not this! These animals would come through that door and snot, spit, and charge whatever was in that pen, to the point that these grown men (who by the way, dressed like I imagined cowboys would, so naturally I assumed they were therefore experienced) would run and hide behind those barricades. When it happened the first time, I thought, "Well, note to self, be careful which cow you acquire." When it happened with nearly every individual animal that came through that pen, I was like, "Well, I guess we aren't raising cattle. But if we're going to be homesteaders and try to minimize our dependency on a grocery store, we're going to have to raise something for meat."

My husband was reminded of a vision he had about being a shepherd. "Well, I can't be a shepherd without sheep."

"Sheep?!" I thought. Yes, sheep.

Sheep are those sweet little creatures David played his harp to. We can raise sheep.

Wait.

I don't know the first thing about sheep.

What do they eat? Will they just stay in the yard? Will this horse fence keep them in? Are there multiple kinds of sheep? What kind of sheep do we need? We did have a farm and certainly can't have a farm without farm animals, so sheep it is.

I read everything I could about sheep, every blog and online book I could access. I found some YouTube shepherds to subscribe to and Facebook groups to join.

In the meantime, dear friends came to visit the farm. Each one would express that such peace came over them even as they approached our fence, before they turned into our driveway. Not one person would leave without saying, unprovoked, what peace they experienced at our place. And we experienced it, too. Peace was tangible when I would drive over the dam on the way home from work. The intensity or magnification of peace grew stronger the closer we got to home. Maybe peace was a location.

Meanwhile, by September, the need for me to visit my grandmother in Florida to aid in navigating medical situations arising from her cancer grew more frequent. I also received the divine revelation that time was short, and we should cherish every moment we had with Gram. When I saw the ad for StoryWorth, it was as if God Himself showed it to me. I asked Gram if she would let me interview her so that I could record her memories for posterity's sake. After all, I didn't know too much about her childhood. Thankfully, she agreed. Once a week, I interviewed her. When I visited her, I interviewed her almost every day I was with her, feverishly copying down every word she said.

At the same time, my husband decided his next right thing was to paint the house. The children went to school in person, which was a huge bonus for them. And I was balancing working from home with days in the office and free time to learn all I could about sheep.

Finally, we were ready to buy our first sheep. We decided to get sheep from three farms and cultivate our flock from there.

We chose dairy sheep. That way, we would have rams for meat, ewes for milk, and wool for warmth. We also bought pregnant sheep; that way we could buy fewer but grow the flock faster.

When the first lambs were born in March 2021, we had sixteen adult sheep on farm. Sixteen became thirty almost overnight with all the lambs that were born.

I'll never forget the moment in March when I woke up and walked from my bedroom to the kitchen looking out toward the barn the whole way, stopped in my tracks, opened the door to the deck, and stepped outside and said, "Oh my goodness, we live on a farm." The sounds were soothing. The view was calming. Not too many days later, I remember being out in the pasture with the sheep, nearly envisioning myself in the pages of the twenty-third Psalm, thinking, "Oh my goodness, I live in Psalm 23. This is that." Maybe rest was a place.

As we dive into the substantive text, we will redefine rest, how to abide there, and why it is possible. I invite you to dispel preconceived notions and open your heart to prepare yourself for a paradigm shift.

ACTIVATION

To enhance your experience, I recommend listening to "Psalm 23 (I Am Not Alone)" by People and Songs, Joshua Sherman, and Steven Musso.

Partner your faith with mine as you read this prayer.

> *Dear Lord, thank You that your desire for me is to abide in Your rest. Teach me Your ways, oh Lord. Reveal to me the areas in my emotions, mind, and spirit that need to be re-calibrated to fall into alignment with my true identity in You. Amen.*

Take a moment to record in your journal, or in the space below, anything that Holy Spirit revealed to you. Also record your hopes, goals, or expected breakthrough as you endeavor to experience *The Gospel IS Rest*.

_____

_____

_____

_____

_____

_____

_____

_____

_____

_____

_____

Some of you may be reading this and you have a lot of "buts" in your mind. But Jesus said, "In this world you will have trouble." But James said, "When you face trials of many kinds," and on and on. So how can you possibly expect me to believe that rest is righteous when we are promised over and over again that we are going to face issues? This book is for you, keep reading.

CHAPTER 2

WHAT IS REST?

WEBSTER'S DICTIONARY DEFINES the noun *rest* as "peace of mind or spirit." It defines the verb *rest*: "to be free from anxiety or disturbance;" "to remain confident: Trust." Conversely, thesaurus.com provides several examples as antonyms for *rest*, including "busyness, clamor, distress, disturbance."

With this initial framework in mind, let's add to it one of our theme verses:

> *"For though the mountains should depart and the hills be shaken or removed, yet My love and kindness shall not depart from you, nor shall My covenant of peace and completeness be removed, says the Lord, Who has compassion on you."* (Isaiah 54:10 AMPC)

I believe that the "easy yoke" and the "light burden" Jesus promised to all who are weary is the embodiment of the divine covenant of peace contained in Isaiah 54:10. To be at rest, to operate from rest, is to embrace this covenant of peace.

GRANDMA KNEW HOW TO REST

I had been flying back and forth to Florida since September. When I was there in February, I knew I needed to get my family to see her as soon as possible, so we made plans to return during spring break.

When we returned as a family, we put jigsaw puzzles together, watched movies, and listened to the Gaithers. We spent time as a family, cherishing every moment.

As often as possible, I asked her another question from the StoryWorth list. I decided to set a goal of 50 questions. I learned many things about my gram, her family, and even about my dad, aunt, and uncles that I hadn't known. I learned funny things about food, mischief, vacations, and adventure.

Through it all, I learned that her story of faith was intricately woven through all of life's facets. I had known, for example, that my uncle dove into a pool and broke his neck when he was nineteen. I had known that my grandmother cared for him his entire adult life. I didn't know that she tangibly experienced God with her from the moment she learned of the tragedy, to the days that she sat in the hospital, through the health struggles that arose years later. Her faith was NEVER shaken. She related:

> The surgeon told us that if he operated on Todd, he would never walk again and would not be able to move his head from side to side. However, he was gonna

help me. I know I wouldn't have gotten through that without the Lord.

There was a whole section at the [University of Michigan Hospital] where people had similar neck injuries, all kinds of different accidents. They all had halos. Todd had his surgery in Missouri. He didn't need a halo. His neck was already stable. That was very encouraging to me that he didn't have the halo on, he didn't have to be in position to look at you, he could move his head around.

There were always small signs that the Lord was with me. The Lord definitely gave me strength. People were amazed at how much strength I had. People would marvel. I knew that God gave me the strength.

"How was it possible?" I wondered. As a mother, I could not imagine keeping a level head if something like that happened to one of my children. How did she rest when everyone around her expected her to fret?

I had known that my other uncle was shot in the eye with a BB gun. I didn't know the testimony of how people prayed and God saved his eyesight. Not only did she remember, there was even a newspaper article she kept that described what happened and the miracle that followed.

I had known that she faced troubles of many kinds while she was home taking care of my uncle and my grandfather was overseas engaged in mission work.

My dad told us that he experienced poverty growing up. From Gram's perspective, notwithstanding lack of funds, her husband (my grandfather) made time for family. As far as food

and meals, God always provided. At every turn, with every example of life events which would be challenging for the most
resilient among us, her faith NEVER wavered.

When I asked her if she had ever doubted her faith, she
looked at me like I had three heads, and she said:

> I don't think that I have ever doubted my faith. I don't
> ever remember blaming the Lord. It all worked out.
> The Lord brought every one of them through. Like
> when Rick hurt his finger, and then he ended up going
> to Bible college. There was never a dull moment. _**I got
> rooted and grounded in my faith**_ pretty young. I never
> even thought about going back on the Lord after I
> got saved. Once I was saved, I was saved. My mother
> would say, 'The Lord got you to the altar and He wants
> to make sure that you're going to stay.'

There were times when I interviewed her that I knew I just
had to share because it would bring right-now-encouragement
to my family. If her faith was NEVER shaken in some of her
darkest moments, we could certainly aspire to remain steadfast
in the things we were facing now. The most poignant of which
was when she related that God was sustaining her even now:

> As I have walked through this cancer, I am reminded
> over and over that the Lord is with me. I really haven't
> been sick. I've been strong. They gave me a few
> months to live, they told me to call hospice in, but
> I haven't had any of that. I don't feel any worse than I
> did before. I just thank God every day that I have the
> health and strength that I do. They say that I have

cancer, but I don't feel like I have cancer. The Lord has really sustained me.

I was amazed. No, I was inspired. This is what "rooted and grounded in faith" really means.

"Maybe rest wasn't a place after all," I thought. I wanted what Grandma had.

WHY IS REST IMPORTANT?

Well, mainly because the enemies of rest—otherwise known as distress, worry, and anxiety, which have become so prevalent—affect us more often.

A January 1, 2022 article in *Monitor on Psychology,* by Ashley Abramson, titled "Burnout and Stress are Everywhere," highlighted recent studies about burnout in American workers.[2]

As in 2020, American workers across the board saw heightened rates of burnout in 2021, and according to APA's 2021 Work and Well-being Survey of 1,501 U.S adults workers, 79% of employees had experienced work related stress in the month before the survey. Nearly 3 in 5 employees reported negative impacts of work-related stress, including lack of interest, motivation, or energy (26%) and lack of effort at work (19%). Meanwhile, 36% reported cognitive weariness, 32% reported emotional exhaustion, and an astounding 44% reported physical fatigue, a 38% increase since 2019.

In a March 11, 2022 article titled "16 Employee Burnout Statistics You Can't Ignore," author Courtney Morrison states:

The World Health Organization (WHO) classifies employee burnout as a 'syndrome conceptualized as resulting from chronic workplace stress that has not been successfully managed.' The WHO lists three main symptoms as: feelings of energy depletion or exhaustion; increased mental distance from one's job or feelings negative towards one's career; reduced professional productivity.[3]

Morrison relies on surveys conducted by others to further emphasize the growing trend of burnout among American workers.

- 75% of workers have experienced burnout, with 40% saying they've experience burnout specifically during the pandemic. (FlexJobs)
- 67% of all workers believe burnout has worsened over the course of the pandemic. (Indeed)

These statistics reveal that we are not resting as God intended. Instead, we are growing sick and tired of being sick and tired. Instead of being able to embrace God's kingdom, we are allowing anxiety to rule and reign in our hearts, minds, and environment around us. We are working to rest instead of working from rest. Let me say it another way by borrowing the song title from Canadian rock band Loverboy: we have an epidemic of "Working for the Weekend," instead of working *from* the weekend.

GOD DESIGNED REST FOR US

Did you know God created Adam and Eve AFTER the work was done and in an environment of rest? You can read about it in Genesis chapter one. Their job was to **_BE_** fruitful and multiply as they dwelt with the Lord. Their job was not to __DO__.[4]

You might be thinking, "What does that mean?" It means that their existence was based on relationship and not tasks. It means that God did not intend us to be consumed with doing and achieving. We were not intended to "do" in order to "become" sons and daughters. He intended for us to rest in *being* His sons and daughters. And out of that identity, do. We were designed to rest in the identity we have in Christ.

Rest is the covenant of peace that God made with us passed down from generation to generation.

Let's take a moment and explore some of the things that God's Word says about rest (emphasis added in each verse):

- "*...**My covenant of peace shall not be removed**,' says the Lord, who has compassion on you.*" (Isaiah 54:10 ESV)

- "*Then Jesus said to them, 'The **Sabbath was made to meet the needs of people,** and not people to meet the requirements of the Sabbath.*'" (Mark 2:27 NLT)

- "*Then Jesus said, '**Let's go** off by ourselves to a quiet place and **rest awhile**.' He said this because there were so many people coming and going that Jesus and his apostles didn't even have time to eat.*" (Mark 6:31 NLT)

- "*Are you weary, carrying a heavy burden? **Come to me. I will refresh your life, for I am your oasis.** Simply join your life with mine. Learn my ways and you'll discover that I'm gentle, humble, easy to please. **You will find refreshment and rest in me.** For all that I require of you will be pleasant and easy to bear.*" (Matthew 11:28-30 TPT)

- "*Then, by constantly using your faith, the life of Christ will* be released deep inside you, and the **resting place of his love** will become the very **source** and **root** of your life." (Ephesians 3:17 TPT)

- "*Because of* **you**, *I know the path of life, as I taste the fullness of joy* **in** **your** *presence. At your right side* **I experience divine pleasures** *for evermore.*" (Psalm 16:11 TPT)

- "**He offers a resting place** *for me in his luxurious love. His tracks take me to an* **oasis of peace** *near the quiet brook of bliss.* **That's where he restores and revives my life.**" (Psalm 23:2-3 TPT) *(The Greek verb "to love" is agapao, which is a merging of two words and two concepts. Ago means "to lead like a shepherd," and pao is a verb that means "to rest." Love is our Shepherd leading us to the place of true rest.)*

- "**The Lord is their [unyielding] strength**, *And He is the fortress of salvation to His anointed.*" (Psalm 28:8 AMP)

- "**You will be the inner strength of all your people.**" (Psalm 28:8 TPT)

- "*For* **I fully satisfy the weary soul**, *and* **I replenish every languishing and sorrowful person.**" (Jeremiah 31:25 AMP)

- "*The Lord replied, I will personally go with you, and* **I will give you rest** *everything will be fine for you.*" (Exodus 33:14 NLT)

(I intentionally exposed you to various translations. Sometimes we think that God's vocabulary and our own are different. I submit to you that God speaks your language. If you can't hear Him in the translation you are currently using, I invite you to consider another one.)

In this sampling of verses, we see that God designed us to

work *from* rest instead of *for* rest. His covenant (which means binding agreement, promise kept under seal[5]) of peace SHALL not be removed. I don't know about you, but when I first read that verse, I was like, "Clearly, I am doing something wrong. Peace is not a constant presence in my life." Then I thought, "Well, His promises are always true, they never fail, He never breaks His end of the deal. So maybe I need to make some changes to experience this covenant."

In Mark chapter 2, the Pharisees were attempting to use the Sabbath as a sword, as if to challenge Jesus' spirituality for healing on the Sabbath, or their perceived violation of the law of rest. Jesus expressed His authority over the Sabbath, over the "rest," advising that rest was created for the benefit of the people and not other way around.

Mark, Matthew, and Paul offer additional perspectives of the rest that come from aligning with Christ and joining Him in the work He is doing.

David also experienced the rest that comes from abiding in Christ. The same was revealed to the prophet Jeremiah and Moses. In Him we find our rest. When we are distracted by our circumstances and forget to abide in His rest, He invites us to come away with Him. He offers us this beautiful divine exchange: we trade our heaviness, our stress, our angst, our load we were not meant to carry for His divine rest.

> "HE OFFERS US THIS BEAUTIFUL DIVINE EXCHANGE: WE TRADE OUR HEAVINESS, OUR STRESS, OUR ANGST, OUR LOAD WE WERE NOT MEANT TO CARRY FOR HIS DIVINE REST."

Let's explore additional biblical evidence that the covenant of peace is meant for us *NOW* (emphasis added to the verses):

- *"So as for you, do not seek what you will eat and what you will drink; **nor have an anxious and unsettled mind.** But [strive for and actively] seek His kingdom, and these things will be given to you as well. **Do not be afraid and anxious little flock, for it is your Father's good pleasure to give you the Kingdom.**"* (Luke 12:29,31-32 AMP)

- *"**Refuse to worry** about tomorrow, but deal with each challenge that comes your way, one day at a time. Tomorrow will take care of itself."* (Matthew 6:34 TPT)

- *"**Pour out all your worries and stress** upon him and leave them there, for he always tenderly cares for you."* (1 Peter 5:7 TPT)

- *"So here's what I've learned through it all: **Leave all your cares and anxieties at the feet of the Lord,** and measureless grace will strengthen you."* (Psalm 55:22 TPT)

- *"**Don't be** pulled in different directions or **worried about a thing. Be saturated in prayer** throughout each day, offering your faith-filled requests before God with overflowing gratitude. Tell him every detail of your life, **then God's wonderful peace** that transcends human understanding, **will guard your heart and mind** through Jesus Christ. **Keep your thoughts continually fixed** on all that is authentic and real, honorable and admirable, beautiful and respectful, pure and holy, merciful and kind. And **fasten your thoughts** on every glorious work of God, praising him always. Put into practice the example of all that you have heard from me and the **God of peace will be with you in all things.**"* (Philippians 4:6-9 TPT)

First of all, we learn that seeking His kingdom triggers His provision. Then, we have several verses imploring us to exchange worry for peace. The descriptions convey that peace is a disciplined decision.

Perhaps Philippians reveals the secret sauce: "saturated in prayer," "with overflowing gratitude," "thoughts continually fixed," and "thoughts fastened." Rest is manifested in the mind through the discipline and habit of abiding in Christ and choosing to focus on the things of God.

In all of these verses, we see that He invites us to exchange seeking provision for seeking the Provider.

Exchange fear of the future for focus on today.

Exchange our chaos for His care.

Exchange our grumbling for His grace.

Exchange being pulled for committed to prayer.

Exchange grief for gratitude.

Exchange pity for peace.

I'll leave it there for now and let you meditate on that. Before you say, "Easier said than done," what if you could practice this exchange in such a way that it became a habit, and that habit became a lifestyle of abiding in a place of rest?

Consider Psalm 27:8 (NLT) as a starting place for your response:

> "My heart has heard you say, 'Come and talk with me.'
> And my heart responds, 'Lord I am coming.'"

ACTIVATION

To enhance your experience, I recommend listening to "Still Waters" by Steph Alessi Muina.

As we wrap up this introduction, in accordance with John 16:13 and Psalm 139:23, pray this prayer with me:

> *Holy Spirit, thank You that You are the Spirit of Truth and that You guide us into all truth [full and complete truth]. We lean into You as You reveal the areas in our lives where we need to partner with You in divine exchange. We echo the words of David from Psalm 139:23: "Search me [thoroughly], O God, and know my heart; Test me and know my anxious thoughts[.]" Thank You, Holy Spirit, for revealing to us the places in our lives and in our thoughts where we are anxious and not resting, where we are fretful and not trusting, where we are seeking provision instead of the Provider, where we are fearful and not focused. In Jesus' name, amen.*

Take out your journal and sit quietly for a moment as you listen to what Holy Spirit may reveal. Write down whatever Holy Spirit brings to mind.

_____

_____

_____

_____

_____

_____

When you're ready, symbolically gather in your hands all of that which Holy Spirit revealed to you, ball it up in your hands, and squeeze it tightly. Decide if you are ready to exchange that mess for what God has for you instead. If you're ready, inhale deeply, then open your hands and drop it at the feet of Jesus as you exhale.

Reread 1 Peter 5:7 and Psalm 55:22. (Pull out your Bible, turn to the previous page, or consider this translation):

> "So, humble yourselves under God's strong hand, and in his own good time he will lift you up. You can throw the whole weight of your anxieties upon him, for you are his personal concern." (1 Peter 5:7 PHILLIPS)

> "Pile your troubles on God's shoulders— he'll carry your load, he'll help you out. He'll never let good people topple into ruin." (Psalm 55:22 MSG)

Now ask Holy Spirit what God is going to give you in exchange.

Write down whatever is revealed.

_____

_____

_____

_____

_____

_____

_____

_____

_____

_____

_____

_____

_____

_____

_____

_____

_____

_____

_____

_____

_____

_____

_____

Begin to thank Him for peace which permeates every corner and crevice of your mind and heart. Continue to thank Him for His perfect love which expels all fear (1 John 4:18 NLT).

Practice Tip: As you partner with Holy Spirit, it will be revealed to you when you attempt or succeed in picking back up those thoughts or emotions that you just laid down. Allow your spirit to be quickened so that you can truly leave them at the feet of Jesus and be strengthened by grace. When you catch yourself thinking in ways contrary to rest, resist the distraction of guilt, shame, and condemnation, and instead determine to consistently abide in Christ. It is going to take some discipline to establish a new habit of restfulness. Keep Psalm 139:23 in front of you as you explore more about the gospel of rest.

CHAPTER 3

CASE STUDIES ON REST

ELIJAH'S STORY

ELIJAH IS ONE of my absolute favorite people in the Bible. In 1 Kings chapter 18, the prophet Elijah met with King Ahab and challenged him to a battle between the Lord God and the god Baal. His plan was that the 450 prophets of Baal would prepare an ox and place it on a wooden altar, and he—Elijah, prophet of the Lord God—would prepare another ox and place it on another altar. Neither altar would be lit with fire. Instead, the prophets of Baal would call on their god and he would call on his God, and whomever answered by fire was the real God.

The people agreed.

It was this giant spectacle. The prophets of Baal carried on all morning and into the afternoon, raising their voices, even cutting themselves, but there was no response.

Elijah prepared his altar by rebuilding the altar of God, which had been torn down by the queen, lining it with twelve stones representing the twelve tribes, digging a trench, and dousing the altar with water three times, filling the trench.[1] He prayed aloud a simple prayer, asking God to reveal Himself so that the people would know that God was truly God. The altar was consumed with fire and the trench filled with water became dry.

All the people fell face downward and proclaimed that the Lord is God.

So then, Elijah told the king that he needed to get up and eat and drink because the rain was coming.[2] Knowing that rain was coming, Elijah urged King Ahab to hurry so he would not get trapped by the rain. Ahab took his chariot to Jezreel and Elijah ran the twenty miles to Jezreel. Elijah beat Ahab to Jezreel. When Ahab told Jezebel, the queen, all that had happened, she threatened Elijah's life. And so, Elijah ran for his life.

Okay, this guy is so grafted to the vine and has such an intimate relationship with the Lord that fire came down from heaven on a soaking wet altar at his request. Then, all the people declared God is Lord. He has such a prophetic anointing that he knows when the rain is coming. And yet, he ran for his life.

Let's pick up in I Kings 19:4:

> *"But he himself traveled a day's journey into the wilderness, and he came and sat down under a juniper tree and asked*

---

1. The water is a separate story in and of itself because they were in the middle of the drought, but let me not get distracted.

2. Immediately following is the story of Elijah's servant going to check for a rain cloud and the 7th time he sees a cloud the size of a man's hand.

[God] that he might die. He said, 'It is enough; now, O Lord, take my life, for I am no better than my fathers.' He lay down and slept under the juniper tree, and behold, an angel touched him and said to him, 'Get up and eat.' He looked, and by his head there was a bread cake baked on hot coal, and a pitcher of water. So he ate and drank and lay down again. Then the angel of the Lord came again a second time and touched him and said, 'Get up, and eat, for the journey is too long for you [without adequate sustenance].' So he got up and ate and drank, and with the strength of that food he traveled forty days and nights to Horeb (Sinai), the mountain of God." (1 Kings 19:4-8 AMP)

I did not leave out any part of this story. He fought and prevailed against the prophets of Baal, he accurately predicted the rain, he probably saved Ahab's life, and he had an expediency anointing such that he won a twenty-mile foot race against a chariot. And yet, he was afraid and depressed. I am convinced that when he prayed that he would die, he truly believed that he would wake up in heaven. I am convinced that he thought he would die.

Notice God's response.

There was no scolding, shame, condemnation, shouting, or earthquake. Instead, ministering angels came to Elijah. They gently woke him from his sleep and brought him food and water.

I love this story because it portrays an incredibly compassionate and practical God. It reveals that the heart of God **is rest.** God does not require us to grind, strive, and strain in our strength. He wants us to rest—rest in His presence, in His abiding peace.

Sometimes God invites us to stop what we are doing and dedicate time to be with Him. Like Jesus did before he walked on water, and before Judas betrayed Him in the garden. In these moments, we are recalibrated and realigned with the abiding rest that comes with being grafted to the vine and partnering with the Lord.

This is why the angel was ministering to Elijah, bringing him food and water and allowing him to rest. We cannot say with certainty how many days he rested and was comforted. But eventually, his instructions were to prepare for what was next. Eventually, the Lord knew Elijah was ready for the next assignment. He wouldn't allow Elijah to quit. And yet, the Lord knew Elijah would need a next level anointing to continue to fulfill his assignment.

Let's pick up where we left off:

> *"There he came to a cave and spent the night in it; and behold, the word of the Lord came to him, and He said to him, 'What are you doing here, Elijah?'*
>
> *"He said, 'I have been very zealous (impassioned) for the Lord God of hosts (armies) [proclaiming what is rightfully and uniquely His]; for the sons of Israel have abandoned (broken) Your covenant, torn down Your altars, and killed Your prophets with the sword. And I, only I, am left; and they seek to take away my life.' So He said, 'Go out and stand on the mountain before the Lord.'*
>
> *"And behold, the Lord was passing by, and a great and powerful wind was tearing out the mountains and breaking the rocks in pieces before the Lord; but the Lord*

was not in the wind. And after the wind, [there was] an earthquake, but the Lord was not in the earthquake. After the earthquake, [there was] a fire, but the Lord was not in the fire; and after the fire, [there was] the sound of a gentle blowing.

"When Elijah heard the sound, he wrapped his face in his mantle (cloak) and went out and stood in the entrance of the cave.

"And behold, a voice came to him and said, 'What are you doing here, Elijah?'

"He said, 'I have been very zealous for the Lord God of hosts (armies), because the sons of Israel have abandoned (broken) Your covenant, torn down Your altars and killed Your prophets with the sword. And I, only I, am left; and they seek to take away my life.'" (1 Kings 19:9-14 AMP)

Do you think that God needed Elijah to repeat himself? Do you think that Elijah thought God didn't hear him the first time? Even though Elijah was comforted and rested, he still wasn't ready to lay down how he felt. This passage reflects a *"Lord, I believe, help my unbelief"* mentality (Mark 9:24), as if Elijah was saying, "I will rest in You; I just need another minute." And even though Elijah's comments didn't reflect a changed mindset, God still wasn't done with Elijah. Not only did Elijah still have an assignment, he had a big assignment. I love verse 15: *"Then the Lord told him, 'Go back the same way you came, and travel to the wilderness of Damascus.'"*

In other words, "GO BACK! Your job is not done, Elijah. You cannot disqualify yourself from My call on your life. I have kings and prophets for you to anoint. Go back, Elijah!"

Here's the beautiful part: Elijah obeyed.

God knows exactly what we need and when we need it. Elijah had an abiding presence of God in his life and knew how to behave from a place of rest. But even he got distracted and disturbed by the circumstances around him and needed to get away to be recalibrated to continue his assignment. Even Jesus, God Himself, dedicated time to just be a Son and abide in the presence of His Father. From these examples, we learn that to operate from a place of rest, we must also consecrate time, and commit to abide in His rest.

JESUS' EXAMPLE

Jesus Himself painted a beautiful picture of rest throughout His ministry. Let us consider Luke 5:16 (TPT): *"But Jesus **often** slipped away from them and went into the wilderness to pray."* And also Luke 22:39 (TPT): *"Jesus left the upper room with His disciples and, **as was his habit**, went to the Mount of Olives, His secret place of prayer."* A secret place, war room, or prayer closet are necessary in our partnership with God. Spending time in these moments definitely contributes to having the abiding rest I am discussing.

Notice the words "often" and "habit." If we want to operate from a position of rest, we must habitually commune often with the Author of rest. I have heard many consider these examples of Jesus a model of a consistent prayer life, and it is that, too. I think it is what some would refer to as a "both, and." It is an example of spending time in prayer and it is also an example of disciplined rest and rejuvenation. How can we possibly operate from rest if we do not spend time with the One whose covenant with us is rest?

I can already hear the excuses: "I have three kids. I work full time. You don't know what my days are filled with. I'm already at the church six days a week and my days are full. I don't have time for anything else." You may have heard it said, "Choose your hard." We can say that it is hard to make rest a discipline. Well, it's really hard, and I may say impossible, to be at peace and effective in life without divine rest.

It is no accident that Paul tells us to *"make your life a prayer"* (1 Thessalonians 5:17 TPT). I believe the Lord has invited us to abide in His rest. This is a lifestyle of setting aside time to pray; undivided, undistracted time soaking in His presence; and praying without ceasing, constantly aware of His abiding presence.

Mark chapter 1 records Jesus preaching, delivering, and healing many. Then we get to verse 35 (TPT): *"The next morning, Jesus got up long before daylight, left the house while it was dark, and made his way to a secluded place to give himself to prayer."* Luke records something similar in chapter 4 verse 42: *"At daybreak the next morning, the crowds came and searched everywhere for him, but Jesus had already left to go to a secluded place..."*

In case you were wondering whether Jesus was fully God and fully man, in my opinion these two verses alone are ample evidence. Jesus needed to recharge His batteries. He disciplined Himself to spend time with His Father.

Jesus challenged us to come to Him when we are tired, weary, or burdened. The lifestyle of rest I am talking about can only be found in Jesus. How can we find that rest but by spending time with Him? If Jesus needed to get away and rest with His Father, how much more do we need to do the same?

Throughout Jesus' ministry, the Bible records a discipline of rest, abiding in the presence of God. He did this before and after ministry. For example, *"One of those days Jesus went out to a mountainside to pray, and spent the night praying to God. When morning came, He called His disciples to Him and chose twelve of them, whom He also designated apostles"* (Luke 6:12-13). The choice of the disciples was most likely not an easy task. Before making the decision, He prayed all night long.

I mentioned that Jesus' example of prayer can also be construed as an example of rest. Mark 6:30-32 (NIV) says, *"The apostles gathered around Jesus and reported to Him all they had done and taught. Then, because so many people were coming and going that they did not even have a chance to eat, He said to them, 'Come with Me by yourselves to a quiet place and get some rest.' So they went away by themselves in a boat to a solitary place."* God is so gracious to use multiple illustrations to confirm His desire for us to rest in Him. The pattern of prayer and rest wasn't just for Jesus. The invitation from Matthew 11:28 is modeled out in Mark 6. How can we come to Him to get rest? We spend time in His presence.

If it is difficult to imagine a way to pray constantly, let's consider an alternative conceptualization. Psalm 1:1-2 records the formula for being blessed, fortunate, prosperous, and favored. It is the formula for operating from rest. Consider verse 2 (AMP): *"But his delight is in the law of the Lord, And on His law [His precepts and teachings] he [habitually] meditates day and night."* The blessed person is a person who enjoys the Word of the Lord and makes it her habit to dwell on what is good and praiseworthy. The Passion Translation describes this as a *"passion to remain true to the Word of 'I AM.'"*

The concept is repeated in Joshua 1:8 (MSG): *"And don't for a minute let this Book of The Revelation be out of mind. Ponder and meditate on it day and night, ensuring you practice everything writ-ten in it."* Instead of allowing whatever comes to mind to gov-ern our thoughts, the Bible instructs us to be purposeful about what we choose to think. Proverbs 4:3 makes this instruction all the more poignant: Be careful what we think about, because thoughts run our life.[6] I submit to you that while the Holy Spir-it initiates rest, it is either advanced or thwarted in the mind. As we choose to make our life a prayer and discipline ourselves to mediate on things above, we make rest a habit.

> "WHEN WE HAVE A LIFESTYLE OF REST AND PEACE, FULLY ABIDING IN THE VINE, WE ARE THEN EQUIPPED TO BE UNSHAKABLE."

When we have a lifestyle of rest and peace, fully abiding in the vine, we are then equipped to be unshakable. For example, when we look at Mark 4:35-41, we find the story of Jesus sleep-ing on a pillow in a boat caught in a terrible storm. The storm is so bad, the men who were fisherman for a living were scared.

> *"And a fierce windstorm began to blow, and waves were breaking over the boat, so that it was already being swamped. But Jesus was in the stern, asleep [with His head] on the [sailor's leather] cushion. And they woke Him and said to Him, 'Teacher, do You not care that we are about to die?' And He got up and [sternly] rebuked the wind and said to the sea, 'Hush, be still (muzzled)!' And the wind died down [as if it had grown weary] and there was [at once] a great calm [a perfect peacefulness]: "Jesus said to them, 'Why are you afraid? Do you still have no faith and confidence [in Me]?' They were filled with great fear, and said to each other, 'Who then is this, that even the wind and the sea obey Him?'"* (Mark 4:37-41 AMP)

Verse 38 in the Passion Translation says it this way: *"But Jesus was calmly sleeping in the stern, resting on a cushion."* The same story is found in Matthew's gospel, in Matthew 8:24 (TPT): *"Suddenly a violent storm developed, with waves so high the boat was about to be swamped. Yet Jesus continued to sleep soundly."*

Jesus knew how to operate from a peace paradigm. And His peace quelled all surrounding chaos, allowing Him to remain steadfast with a sound mind. Jesus' model should inspire each of us. When we are purposeful to consecrate time in His presence and heed the words of Paul for our life to be a prayer, what we're doing is partnering with God in creating an environment of abiding rest. What kind of inner peace, what kind of abiding rest, must Jesus have had to remain undaunted by the circumstances that were so disturbing and distressing to those around Him?

Let's look at another example. This time, Jesus walks on water in the storm. The story is found in John 6, Matthew 14, and Mark 6.

> *"Seeing the disciples straining at the oars, because the wind was against them, at about the fourth watch of the night (3:00-6:00 a.m.) He came to them walking on the sea."* (Mark 6:48 AMP)

> *"By now a strong wind began to blow and was stirring up the waters. The disciples had rowed about halfway across the lake when all of a sudden they caught sight of Jesus walking on top of the waves, coming toward them."* (John 6:18-19 TPT)

> *"But the disciples, who were now in the middle of the lake, ran into trouble, for their boat was tossed about by the high winds and heavy seas. At about four o'clock in the morning,*

Jesus came to them, walking on the waves!" (Matthew 14:24-25 TPT)

Living from a posture of rest, abiding in His peace, includes acknowledging His authority and the authority we have through Him. Not only did Jesus demonstrate that His presence is such that we can *be* peace **in** the middle of disturbing circumstances, we also have the authority to trample **on** the circumstances.

Jesus modeled rest, taking moments of solitude in prayer, going away with His closest friends to pray together, and exuding rest notwithstanding tumultuous situations. He wasn't anxious when the disciples perceived there wasn't enough food to feed the multitudes, He wasn't daunted by the demonic spirits, and the stormy seas didn't faze Him. He maintained His authority in the middle of circumstances He did not change and over situations He ultimately did change. Jesus' model is one of resting in both the identity and the authority of God. When we abide in Christ and He in us (John 15:4), we too can rest in the identity and the authority of Almighty God.

ONE OF MY EXPERIENCES WITH OPERATING FROM REST

God's presence and sustaining grace were tangible as our family walked through our grandmother's graduation to heaven. I would say it felt a lot like the abiding presence the Israelites were provided in the wilderness:

> *"The angel of God, who had been [with us in Florida], moved and went behind [us]. The pillar of the cloud moved from in front and stood behind [us]." (Exodus 14:19, modified)*

Gram obtained her eternal reward on May 19, 2021. She was

laid to rest on May 27, 2021. I returned home after weeks away on May 29, 2021. Within the two weeks that followed, we learned that my dad's illness was more serious than we thought. He didn't need antibiotic for an ear infection and didn't need an adjustment to his blood pressure medication. Instead, various tests, hospital visits, and meetings with doctors revealed that likely he needed surgery on his mastoid that only a few surgeons in the U.S. were skilled enough to perform.

By Friday, June 11, 2021, we arranged for my parents to fly with my sister, Ericka, to her home and I would pick them up from the airport on Tuesday, June 15. One such surgeon, whom my dad had grown to trust, practiced near Ericka's home, less than three hours from me.

In the meantime, on Sunday, June 13, 2021, my husband got a call that he needed to get to Michigan on the next plane because his sister wasn't expected to make it. We knew that she was battling leukemia, but thought she was winning the fight. She had already made plans to care for her yet-to-be born twin grandsons in the fall. But there were complications. We decided that he would go alone and I would stay behind to go to my father.

God sent angels in the form of people from our church to help with our children. Because of everything that I had just intimately experienced with Gram, I could provide emotional and psychological support for my husband even from afar. I could explain the words of the doctors, the next things to be expected, and how to pray very specifically.

As planned, I drove to the airport on Tuesday, June 15, 2021, to retrieve my father, mother, and sister.

While I was en route, I felt like I knew I could not continue to work and care for my family simultaneously. Despite my long absence from the office caring for Gram, I knew I had to make the call that I could not continue to juggle work and family. To this point, I had been juggling working as a full-time lawyer, partner at my firm, supervising more than ten attorneys, and supporting staff, all while simultaneously caring for my family.

I expected the call to be my resignation. Instead, my office said they had cleared my schedule for a month! I was instructed to take care of my family and let them know when I was ready to return. And I would be paid my normal salary for the duration. WOW! God went before me.

As I was driving, I was praying. The FaceTime and phone encounters with my father, mother, and doctors from the last two weeks were weighing heavy on me. While I didn't understand what was wrong with him—and so far, the doctors didn't either; they just had a best guess—I *knew* my father needed a miracle. I had my worship music on and declared health and wholeness over my father. I was releasing Psalm 27:13 over him: "*He will see the goodness of God in the land of the living.*" I was releasing Isaiah 40:31: "*He will walk and not faint.*" I was declaring Jeremiah 33:6: "*You will bring complete health and healing to Him.*" "*It is finished*" (John 19:30). "*By Your stripes [my dad] was healed*" (Isaiah 53:5).

And then my phone rang. My husband called to let me know that his sister was now with Jesus. I was torn. I felt like I needed to be with him; he was broken. And I knew my family was counting on me to come.

"I'll take the next plane from Springfield," I offered. "I can be there tomorrow."

"No. Stick with the plan. Go to your dad," he insisted softly.

"Let me just check on flights and see how soon I can get

there."

"Get to your dad and tell me when you have him."

It was a pretty brief call.

I checked flights anyway. There were none that I could make that afternoon, so I decided to go to my dad and reconsider flying out in the morning.

Now my prayers were not only prayers for health for my father, they included supernatural comfort for my husband and his family.

How could both of these tragedies be happening at the same time?

Yet, somehow, I had peace. I was not feeling frantic.

That was a gift my husband gave me, affirming that I was still doing the right thing by getting to my father. "Lord, heal my father. Comfort my husband. Guard the hearts of my mom and my sister. Do what only You can do."

Suddenly, what dropped in my spirit was not a confirmation or affirmation of my prayers of healing for my father. Instead, I heard, "*Unless a kernel of wheat falls to the ground and dies, it abides alone, but if it dies it produces much fruit.*"

I attempted to disregard this and went back to praying. I turned my music up louder and prayed all the more fervently. "Thank You, Jesus, for healing my father, giving doctors supernatural wisdom, and causing every cell in his body to line up with Your Word. Thank You, Jesus, that You complete the work that You start in us. I thank You for completing the healing that I know You have already paid for in my dad."

For the second time, I didn't feel or hear any "yes" answer to my prayer. Instead, almost silence, as if my prayers were hitting the roof of my car and not going any farther. And again, as if there was a passenger in my car, I heard, "*Unless a kernel of wheat falls to the ground and dies, it abides alone, but if it dies it produces much fruit.*"

This time, I turned my music off and started driving faster. I began to voice text every prayer partner I knew. "I was praying for my dad and I felt like I heard the Lord say, '*Unless a kernel of wheat falls to the ground and dies, it abides alone, but if it dies it produces much fruit.*' What does it mean? Can you pray with me for the interpretation?"

I was instantly reminded that the last time the Lord gave me such a verse was when a dear friend died when I was in high school. He had been the captain of his all-state wrestling team and was a national champion multiple times, but he somehow contracted spinal meningitis and died suddenly. At his funeral, the students and faculty from his school and people from his community and surrounding communities could not fit in the church and crowded around the doors and windows outside. Countless people were saved on that day because of the life testimony of my friend. It was the verse his family chose to put on the bulletin and the one his mother shared with me when she felt the Lord comforting her in her grief.

But surely, death isn't what it means this time. Right? My father is a missionary to Italy. He's a hero and role model to my son, girls, niece, and nephews. He's only sixty-three. He's got a lot more assignment left.

Now, I was shouting my prayers. "Heal my dad! I rebuke sickness and disease and the spirit of death! I release complete wholeness, health, and vitality. JESUS! I believe that You are the Healer. I have more than a mustard seed faith about this. I know his congregation in Italy and online church around the world have way more than mustard seed faith. I know You are going to honor the fervent prayers of Your righteous people."

This time, I can only describe it as a broken record, sounds which could not be drown out by my music or my prayers, overlapping segments of *"Unless a kernel of wheat, unless a kernel of wheat falls to the ground and dies, it abides alone, it abides alone... but if it dies... but if it dies... but if it dies... it produces much fruit."*

"OKAY!" I shouted. "I hear You. But not today, right?"

"No, not today. But sooner than you would like."

"But not today?"

"Not today."

Lord, have mercy, I thought, then quickly whispered, "Well, You'll have to tell Mom and my sisters. I'm not telling them this."

"Not today."

Sigh. Okay. Well, a day is like a thousand years, right? So maybe this is just preparing me for some future event, some far in the future event.

Now I was within forty-five minutes of the airport and my attention shifted to becoming mentally prepared to be whatever was needed for whatever we would encounter when I got to the airport.

In the supernatural, I was reapplying the armor. I prayed for mental clarity and wisdom beyond my years (helmet); I prayed that garrison peace would guard my heart (breastplate); I prayed for expeditious receipt of accurate information (belt); I prayed for traveling mercies and His abiding presence to be with us at every turn (sandals).

They landed.

I let my mom know I was at the airport. She asked that I park and come in. *What? Why? My parents have flown millions of times.*

They have my sister with them to help.

Silently, I prayed, "Jesus. Jesus. Jesus..."

The man I encountered at that airport was not the one I had left in Florida two weeks earlier. This man was shuffling his feet, head bowed, watching his feet as he traversed the lobby of that airport assisted by my mother and my sister, one at each side. Silently, I continued to pray, "Jesus. Jesus. Jesus..." I was not prepared for this. And yet, I continued to have mental energy and peace.

We had ordered take out and grabbed it on the way to Ericka's home. We agreed as a family that we would eat a meal, go to bed, then take my father to the hospital in the morning. As we were sitting at the table eating dinner, my father had what appeared to be a seizure. Before I realized what I was doing, I was outside. My mom soon joined me and encouraged me not to freak out. I wasn't freaking out; I was just realizing that our plan to wait until morning was probably not best. If this was a seizure, or worse, a stroke, he needed a doctor, now. Dad wanted to stick to the plan.

Mom knew to call the doctor with whom they had spoken just last week. He was the one who would perform the anticipated surgery.

He answered.

Dad wanted to speak with him.

The doctor immediately knew that this wasn't the same man he had spoken with even the week prior. He advised my father that he needed to go directly to the Emergency Room, that this could not wait until morning.

Resigned, Dad agreed.

I don't know how many tests were run or labs drawn in those

first couple days at the hospital. But we quickly learned that this was not a stroke or a seizure. A couple different antibiotics and steroids were administered while we continued to wait for more test results. We asked the doctors if we needed to get my sister Jessica from California, and when the answer was yes, I felt like that conversation with God in the car was preparation for *THIS*. When we called Jessica, she was at kids' camp. She recalled just seeing my father at Grandma's funeral. She knew that he was "grieving," but he was fine. She couldn't hear our urgency.

We called my brother-in-law.

Jessica was on her way.

I left my mom and Ericka at the hospital and picked Jessica up at the airport. In the car en route, my mom called to tell me to please hurry, Dad was praying prayers of blessing over each family member and my mom didn't know what that meant.

"Not today. Right, Lord?" I prayed in my spirit.

"Not today."

I felt confirmed by the Spirit.

I called my husband and told him he would need to come and make arrangements to bring the children. I related the "kernel of wheat" experience I had en route. He agreed to come the next day.

I got Jessica to the hospital. Miraculously, the hospital allowed all of us to stay with my dad. We didn't all stay all the time; we took turns returning to Ericka's home to shower and rest. But my father was never alone.

My sisters pleaded with my father, "Did you tell God to heal you?" His response was only a whisper, "We don't tell God, we ask Him. Pray Jesus' prayers." We knew that he meant for us all to pray, "Thy will be done." My father's faith seemed giant-sized not only in the healing power of God, but also in His sovereignty.

Even though his condition continued to deteriorate, his faith never wavered. Even when he began to need assistance with the basics of life, he still knew how to access the throne room (Hebrews 4:16).

On Friday night, he laid hands on his head as he called down heaven:

> *The battle is the Lord's. No weapon formed against you can prosper. Sickness, you're under my feet. I pray in the name that's above every name that the virtue of God flow into my brain cells. The lifter of my head, of my spirit and knowledge of God, God bring clarity of thought to my mind. Bring clarity of thought to my brain, every avenue, every category.*
>
> *God, refresh, steal back what the enemy has stolen. Rise up in victory. I defeat you, enemy, in the name of Jesus. Sickness, you have no place here; sickness, I defeat you in Jesus' name. You have to come under the authority of speaking the name of Jesus. Submit, enemy of my soul and my spirit. Sickness, be defeated. Cancer, be defeated. God, I pray in Jesus' name, Your Word says by Your stripes we are healed, body, mind, soul, and spirit. Be healed in Jesus' name. Rise up in Jesus' name. Be delivered in Jesus' name.*
>
> *No weapon will stand against You. Lord, You have the final word in my life. Lord, I give You full reign in my life, full control. Sickness, you're defeated. Cancer, you're defeated. Be defeated, enemy, in Jesus' name.*
>
> *God, bless Your church in Rome. Let its greatest year*

be this year. Let the most souls be saved this year. Let the sons and daughters rise up in victory. Let them see the soldiers marching on in victory. God, give them strength, renew their strength. Let them see this as a victory. Let them see it in their mind's eye, the spirit eye, that says we are more than conquerors, no weapon formed against us can prosper.

Enemy, you are defeated. Sickness, you are defeated. Rise up, awake, oh Israel. Awake, oh man of God. Rise up, Spirit of the living God. Set free the captive, release sickness, defeat sickness, in the name of Jesus, in the name that's above every name.

I speak life to my mind. I speak life to my brain. You have no place of authority in my mind in the name of Jesus Christ. Refreshed, our minds renewed, our spirit man renewed, we will walk in victory and in triumph.

Enemy, you are defeated. You are under our feet. Sickness has no place nor authority in this home. Be defeated, enemy, I pray in the name of Jesus.

Lord, we stand in awe of You. We are amazed at Your glory. We are amazed at Your wonder. We are Your chosen. You have hand-picked us. We will fulfill the responsibilities that You have set before us. Hallelujah to the Lamb of God. Blessed be Your name.

I had often reminded myself that even when David was greatly distressed, he encouraged himself in the Lord (1 Samuel 30:6). This thing I witnessed with my father took that verse to a whole new level. This man needed assistance with the simplest of tasks and yet he laid hands on his head and prayed us all into the holy of holies.

That Friday night was not the only time my father engaged the prophetic. On Father's Day morning, my husband had some moments alone with my dad, and asked if my dad had anything he wanted to say. As my husband began to record, my father said, "Unless a kernel of wheat fall to the ground and dies..."

He sent me the video while I was with my mom and sisters at church.

I knew I needed to tell my mom.

As I began to tell my mom that I needed to tell her something, she nearly interrupted me to tell me she needed to tell me something, too. You see, my father's last sermon was "Ready for the Trumpet," and as he was preaching that message, my mother was sitting on the front row when she heard my father explain how close he was to eternity. At the time, she had just made a mental note that was odd to convey in the middle of the sermon. But now, she felt like that sermon was God's way of preparing her for what was to come. As we exchanged stories, we both agreed it didn't necessarily mean anything imminent, and we would continue to pray for health and vitality. Also, we would deal with what is and begin to make plans if the current trajectory didn't change.

I can't explain to you how sufficient grace sustained me. I could simultaneously hope and pray—and plan in case God didn't heal my dad on this side of heaven.

My dad didn't want to be in the hospital in the first place, much less die there, so I knew we had to get him out of there. But in a COVID-era, any rehab center or nursing home required quarantine. I called every one. And every one required at least two weeks of quarantine, and even then, most wouldn't allow our family to be with him.

Okay, Holy Spirit, what do You have in store here? Lead me.

A lady at the hospital didn't know anything about it, but she had heard of this place, Jacob's Ladder, and suggested I call them. When I called, Camila agreed to meet me that same day. When I arrived at this house, it looked like someone's home. It didn't appear sterile or institutional. It didn't look like a medical facility. She opened the front door as I approached and gently said, "God sent you to me." She showed me around and explained that they could house four patients at a time, but for whatever reason, the last couple of people who had inquired, she had declined. She explained that these services were free, donation only, and if we agreed to allow her to care for my father, she would receive no one else while we were there. She had room for all of us so we could remain with him as long as we wanted.

In the ten days my dad was at the hospital, his prognosis went from one year, to several months, to a couple months, to several weeks, and finally to two weeks when we as a family finally agreed to engage hospice. My sisters and I all had our husbands by our sides and my mother had her sister-cousins (as she calls them) by hers. Even my father's two best friends were there. The hospital chaplain and his wife attributed their being in the ministry to my father's influence on their lives and they, too, supported us while we were receiving earth-shattering news.

There are not enough pages to express the eternal gratitude we have for those who dropped what they were doing and just sat with us for days. We were never alone. As God did for Moses, Jehovah Nissi hovered over all of us, and God sent us Aarons and Hurs to help hold up our arms during this time.

Ultimately, modern medicine had reached its limits, and now it was time to allow God to do what only He could. My father was transferred to Jacob's Ladder.

Camilia's assistant Lydia was an angel from heaven. She prepared meals and snacks and wouldn't take no for answer as she insisted we needed to eat. She cleaned every day and handled laundry. All the while, she played soft angelic music through the built-in sound system. When we tried to thank them, they said their assignment was to care for the man of God (my father) and his family.

My dad went to be with Jesus the Sunday after Father's Day, his favorite day of the week. And all of us were with him. In our darkest moments, God was there.

From the time I began driving to Springfield to the day of his celebration of life service, I experienced a new dimension of "dwelling in the secret place" and "abiding under the shadow of the Almighty." It brought completely new insight to the concept of abiding IN Christ and He in us, and being grafted to the vine.

That's not to say there wasn't an indescribable ache in my heart and innumerable tears shed. There were. But peace abounded.

MY OWN CAVE EXPERIENCE

In this chapter, we talked about when Elijah found himself under the tree, he had not completed his assignment.

We talked about how God was gracious to provide rest and rejuvenation for him and gave Elijah a fresh anointing, equipping him to complete the assignment.

God did something similar for me. He didn't lead me to an

actual cave in the cleft of rock, but He gave me a vision. This was particularly interesting for me because I am not one to have visions or dreams. Normally, God speaks to me through His Word or quickens me in my Spirit. I believe that God gave me this experience because next level assignments require next level encounters with God.

I was at home getting ready, when all of a sudden, it was like a screen came down and I saw a roomlike cave or underground room where people were dressed in camouflage, like a military.

> *I saw a message passed like a scratch piece of paper grip to grip. It was read and, immediately, the entire room stood to attention. Their movements were swift and also deliberate, as they marched by the armory cabinet.*
>
> *It was impossible to tell how many were there because the sound of the steps was deafening and wholly in unison as one thunderous footstep at a time. Each soldier was handed two weapons: a rifle and a handgun.*
>
> *It was as if a narrator was describing the scene for me: This was not their first day of training. This was after years or decades of training. What they have gone through to be that prepared for the message, how they have trained and sweat and cried, how they have bled and fought and died to be ready. Ready for this mission. They have waited, and in their waiting, prepared for this day. They have waited, and in their waiting, they have trained for this message. They have known. They were taught that this day would come and yet they have waited. But they did not fall asleep. No, they recognized the waiting was the only opportunity for training and developing and strategizing.*

They recognized that the waiting was the only time to sharpen their swords and acquire more ammunition. They recognized that the waiting was the only time to train their minds for battle, to discipline themselves to be slave to the spirit and not to the flesh.

This was not their first battle, but this was the battle that they had been preparing for and they were READY. Are you?

I heard the Lord say, Why do you look at your life in reverse? How did you not know that this was all conditioning for your future? You said "this is all I can take" and it was a mark about your waist, and yet you overcame an onslaught that was about sternum high and now you have been conditioned to withstand an even greater test. You know the testing of your faith produces perseverance, and perseverance character.

I felt like I was drinking from a fire hose. I felt admonished and challenged. In much the same way that God ministered to Elijah and then reiterated Elijah's calling, I felt God doing that for me. He sustained me during the biggest test of my life, then comforted me supernaturally by His Spirit. Then He gave me a vision to reignite His call on my life. He affirmed that this trial, this juniper tree experience of grief, would not be the end. Instead, it would be a launching pad for the greater things to come. Maybe He wouldn't have me anoint kings, but He made clear my assignment wasn't finished.

I have had other moments when I felt God call or seal my calling. What was different in this experience from the previous ones was that this time I not only knew I wasn't being asked to do anything in my strength, I was admitting that I *couldn't* do it in my strength. I was done grinding, striving, and straining. I felt I had nothing left to give. This was going to be a new kind of rest.

Matthew 5:3 (MSG) became my new motto: *"You're blessed when you're at the end of your rope. With less of you there is more of God and his rule."*

It was in that "cave" that I truly realized that I *belong* to a kingdom not of this world. I felt quickened in my spirit, that there is a warfare that cannot be expressed in English human terms. It is important to recognize that the enemy of our soul is relentless. He takes different tactics and wears different clothes, but we must call it for what it is and rebuke and push it back. We have the authority to bind and loose in the spirit. We must remember that our battle is not against flesh and blood but against powers and principalities of the dark world. We must fight supernatural enemies with supernatural power. Failing to identify the enemy, thinking the situation is natural, fighting/dealing with/handling it in our strength and human wisdom... this all fails to give Holy Spirit space to do His work.

We must keep the armor on, every single piece, and be consciously aware of the use and purpose of each piece. The devil's schemes are cunning and intentionally camouflaged. We must see with our spiritual sight. We must recognize that we belong to a kingdom not of this world. We are co-heirs of that kingdom with all authority and the same power that raised Jesus from the dead. We must not shrink back or give in, not one inch. We must purpose to walk in THAT authority and embrace the VICTORY in that realm regardless of what it looks like in the natural.

When we're tired, when we're mourning, when we're distracted, it takes uncompromising discipline to take captive every thought, every emotion, and declare only the goodness of God over our lives and our circumstances. In these moments, we must guard our tongues and not allow the enemy to use our words to gain any foothold. Our tongues hold the power of life and death. When we are weary, we must purpose to be disciplined to bridle our tongues.

I believe that THIS TOO shall pass, and when it does, we will find ourselves on another level with more strength, power, and peace. This is not the time to relent, but to press in and press up. God does have this, but we must not get in His way by attempting to handle "the things" without Him.

With the newfound resolve that I have the God-given authority to bind and to loose, I began to loose and to bind. (As you read these next sentences, I encourage you to bind your faith with mine and bind and loose in agreement.)

I loose supernatural strength, discernment, and wisdom.

I loose peace that passes understanding and joy unspeakable and full of glory.

I bind every tactic, thought, and emotion not given by God, tear down every stronghold, and rebuke every attempted advance of the enemy.

I loose health and vitality, abundance and financial provision, more than we have asked, can contemplate, or even imagine.

I loose clarity of mind and thought and supernatural creativity.

I loose supernatural acceleration anointing for all of the

things; God's time table, supernaturally expeditious.

I loose unity, a bond unbreakable, non-penetrable in our families, parents/children, husbands/wives, and siblings.

I decree and declare this season over and the new one of harvest and breakthrough and next level anointing begun in Jesus' name.

For me, the cave experience, after the grief tree, left me with the determination that: As for me, I do not belong to those who shrink back or are held back, but my confident trust is in Him (Hebrews 10:39). I will hope in Him (Lamentations 3:24). I will abide in Him (John 15:4). In that cave, I learned rest is most definitely an operating system.

ACTIVATION

If you like the addition of worship with the activation, I invite you to listen to "Trust in God" by Steven Furtick, Chris Brown, Brandon Lake, and Mitch Wong.

1. Reread 1 Kings 19:4.

Have you ever found yourself trying to remove yourself from your situation(s) or hiding from God? Are you there now? What if you gave God a moment to be for you what He was to Elijah? What would it look like if you were honest with God about how you're truly feeling about Him, your situation, and yourself? Pull out your journal and write down the first things that come to mind.

_____

_____

_____

_____

_____

_____

2. Reread 1 Kings 19:5-14.

Are you in a season of rest or preparation? Is it time to begin your next assignment? Write down your answer to that question. Write your own name in the blank below before asking yourself the next question aloud:

What are you doing here, _____? Write down your answer.

_____

_____

_____

_____

_____

_____

Ask Holy Spirit if it's time to rest, time to prepare, or time to get back to your assignment.

Ask Holy Spirit to reveal to you the answer to these questions: "How does God see me? How does God see my situation? What would He have for me to do?"

Take a few moments as you listen to what Holy Spirit may reveal to you. Write down whatever Holy Spirit brings to mind.

_____

_____

_____

_____

_____

_____

3. Read Hebrews 10:39; Lamentations 3:24; and John 15:4. As you read the verses, write down a word or phrase that seems to jump off the page at you.

_____

_____

_____

_____

_____

_____

Read the verses again. Is it the same word or phrase that jumps out to you this time? What do you observe? What do you notice about any particular word(s), phrase(s), or verse(s)? What do you think the main message is for you today?

_____

_____

_____

_____

_____

Read the verses a third time and ask Holy Spirit how to apply this truth to your life. Are there any changes you need to make in the way you think, speak, or act?

_____

_____

_____

_____

_____

_____

Now turn these thoughts into prayer. Ask Holy Spirit to show you how to meditate on and apply this truth to your life. Record your prayer to refer to later.

_____

_____

_____

_____

_____

_____

_____

_____

_____

_____

_____

_____

_____

_____

_____

_____

_____

_____

_____

_____

_____

_____

_____

_____

PART TWO

I'm sold. I'm ready for a new operating system. I want to abide in rest and live from rest. How do I do that? How can I recalibrate and reprogram myself to live from, not for the weekend? What do I need to change about my attitude, thought process, and behavior to make rest a reality?

In this section, we will walk through practical steps to make tweaks in our mindsets and changes to our default positions so that we can begin to abide in rest as God intended.

CHAPTER 4

BE STILL AND KNOW

HOW TO LIVE FROM A PLACE OF REST

L IVING FROM REST begins with Psalm 46:10: *"Be still and know that I am God."* There is so much packed into this seemingly basic instruction. "Be still" is even more intense than the serenity prayer. It's recognizing that there is much beyond our ability to control. Our job is often just to remain steadfast.

"Be still" combined with "and know" is another way of saying "know your role" and "know what your role isn't." It is to know your assignment distinguished from God's role. "And know" is multifaceted. It is to know who you are and who your God is.

The Great I AM may not occupy His rightful position in

your life. You may have relegated Him to an inferior position, over which you retain authority. There may be areas over which you have yet to ascribe Him Lordship.

"Be still and know" connotes acquiring a corrected understanding of who God is and who you are. I think we are often aware that we do not have a complete or accurate view of God. I think we are less often aware that we don't have a complete or accurate view of ourselves. "Be still and know" means that we come to terms with who God is to us and who we are to Him.

This first step is so critical, it will take two chapters for us to fully explore it together. For now, we will examine three Old Testament examples of this posture of stillness.

Our first example is found in Exodus 14, where the Israelites were fleeing the Egyptians and were approaching the Red Sea. The Israelites thought they were trapped. As promised, Holy Spirit put words in Moses' mouth:

> *"Then Moses said to the people, 'Do not be afraid! Take your stand [be firm and confident and undismayed] and see the salvation of the Lord which He will accomplish for you today; for those Egyptians whom you have seen today, you will never see again. The Lord will fight for you while you [only need to] keep silent and remain calm.'"* (Exodus 14:13-14 AMP)

This seems to be an instance where Moses had faith and doubted simultaneously, because in the next verse, it records the Lord saying, "Why are you crying out to me?" And then God reminded Moses that Moses already had the anointing for this assignment. (See Exodus 4:1-5.) Moses already had the staff, and God gave him fresh instructions for using it during this part of the journey.

"'And the Egyptians shall know [without any doubt] and acknowledge that I am the Lord, when I am glorified and honored through Pharaoh, through his war-chariots and his charioteers.' The angel of God, who had been going in front of the camp of Israel, moved and went behind them. The pillar of the cloud moved from in front and stood behind them." (Exodus 14:18-19 AMP)

Moses did his part by lifting his staff over the water, believing God would make a way, and God did the rest.

The Israelites crossed on dry ground. The Egyptians followed.

Once the Israelites made it safely across, then Moses again raised his staff over the water, and the sea went back to its place and the Egyptians drowned.

"When Israel saw the great power which the Lord had used against the Egyptians, they feared the Lord [with reverence and awe-filled respect], and they believed in the Lord, and in His servant Moses." (Exodus 14:31 AMP)

Moses and the Israelites only needed to continue doing what they were doing. Moses was to remain steadfast. He already knew that the staff was the equipment he needed to lead the children of Israel out of Egypt. God did not bring them this far for their way to be blocked by the Red Sea. We do what we know to do, what God equipped and anointed us to do; we remain in our assignment and He does the rest.

It is times like these when we must remain resolute in the waiting. We discipline ourselves to "be still," while we position ourselves to receive the instructions. In this posture, our spiritual batteries are charged as we allow the Holy Spirit to prepare us for what's next. *"I wait [patiently] for the Lord, my soul [expectantly] waits, And in His word do I hope."* (Psalm 130:5 AMP). In these moments of stillness, I urge you to hope in the words of Isaiah the prophet:

> *"But those who wait for the Lord [who expect, look for, and hope in Him] Will gain new strength and renew their power; They will lift up their wings [and rise up close to God] like eagles [rising toward the sun]; They will run and not become weary, They will walk and not grow tired."* (Isaiah 40:31 AMP)

Another illustration of "be still and know," is found in 2 Chronicles 20. God gave King Jehoshaphat a message through the prophet Jahaziel, similar to the one He had given Moses in Exodus 14. You see, three armies had come together to wage war against Judah. Not only did the king seek the Lord, he proclaimed a fast throughout the kingdom and all the people of Judah sought the Lord. On behalf of his kingdom, he prayed, *"We do not know what to do, but our eyes are on You"* (2 Chronicles 20:12).

"WE DO WHAT WE KNOW TO DO, WHAT GOD EQUIPPED AND ANOINTED US TO DO; WE REMAIN IN OUR ASSIGNMENT AND HE DOES THE REST."

Learning how to live from a position of rest means that we must admit when we do not know what to do. It means that we have to recognize the moment that we are in. "Be still and know" begins with being still; before going to the battlefield, before taking the next step, before doing anything, we are still. Simultaneously, we acknowledge and confess that we wholly rely on God's directions for the next steps. Something amazing happens when we do that: God is faithful to answer us. Look at His response to King

Jehoshaphat's prayer:

> "Be not afraid or dismayed at this great multitude, for the
> battle is not yours, but God's... You need not fight in this
> battle; take your positions, stand and witness the salvation
> of the Lord who is with you, O Judah and Jerusalem. Do
> not fear or be dismayed; tomorrow go out against them, for
> the Lord is with you." (2 Chronicles 20:15, 17 AMP)

I absolutely love this: #notyourjob. The battle is not yours.
It is above your pay grade. The battle is the Lord's. You do not
need to fight. It is not for you to "do." You must "be" grafted to
the vine and remain steadfast. The Lord is with you.

HALLELUJAH! There is a distinction: God's job versus our
job. His job to **do**, our job to **be**. It is so important for us to lean
into the Holy Spirit to recognize what our job is and what it
isn't, so that we can acknowledge and expect God to do His job.

Like Moses did his part and raised his staff as instructed, King
Jehoshaphat also showed up and conducted himself as he believed God instructed him. He told his people, *"Believe and trust
in the Lord your God"* (2 Chronicles 20:20). Then he sent people IN FRONT OF the army who sang praises and gave thanks
to the Lord. King Jehoshaphat recognized praise and worship
as keys to unlocking kingdom authority. What we do in the
waiting is very important. Communing with the Lord through
praise and worship is a great waiting strategy.

"Be still and know" means that we do as God instructs even
when it doesn't make sense. God delivered King Jehoshaphat
from his enemies that day; his enemies ended up killing one
another.

> "And the fear of God came on all the kingdoms of those
> countries when they heard that the Lord had fought against

the enemies of Israel. So the kingdom of Jehoshaphat was quiet, for his God gave him rest on all sides." (2 Chronicles 20:29-30 AMP)

I recognize that with these two examples, some of you are reading this and thinking, "I do not have a prophet that speaks to me with these clear instructions. I don't have a burning bush or a pillar of fire or smoke through which I hear the voice of the Lord like Moses did."

You may think, "This is supposed to be the 'how to' portion of this book and I just don't think it pertains to me." To you I say, bear with me.

Hearing God isn't as difficult and cryptic as we sometimes make it out to be. Sometimes, hearing God is just a peace. Sometimes, it is just a knowing. Sometimes, God speaks through nature. Sometimes, God uses people. Often, He uses His Word.

In the first example, God spoke directly to Moses. In the second example, the prophet spoke to King Jehoshaphat. In this third example, Jonathan simply had a knowing and then he received confirmation. In 1 Samuel 14, the Israelites found themselves surrounded by the Philistines. And only King Saul and his son Jonathan had swords and spears (1 Samuel 13:22).

"One day Jonathan the son of Saul said to his young armor bearer, 'Come, let us go over to the Philistine garrison on the other side.' But he did not tell his father… Jonathan said to his young armor bearer, 'Come, let us cross over to the garrison of these uncircumcised men; it may be that the Lord will work for us. For there is nothing to prevent the Lord from saving, whether by many or by few.'" (1 Samuel 14:1, 6 AMP)

There are three important points in this introduction to our third example. First of all, Jonathan knew who his confidant was. He told his armor bearer but did not tell his father. (Please don't hear what I am not saying. You have to read 1 Samuel 13 to understand who Saul was before you start equating your parents to Jonathan's. Often, God uses our parents to speak into our lives or to confirm what God is speaking to us.) I'm not emphasizing kinship here; I'm highlighting relationships in the broader sense. We must know the difference between co-laborers with Christ, spiritual authority, or accountability and naysayers. Timing is everything here. (Even Job knew when he could not listen to his wife. See Job 2:9-10.)

Secondly, Jonathan recognized that he was made for community. Even though this story reveals only one confidant, Jonathan had the good sense not to go alone. It is a trick of the enemy to isolate us. Don't fall for it.

Have you ever shouted at the TV when the soon-to-be victim was en route to some place alone? It was obvious that this was how she was putting herself in a position to be victimized, or when a policeman pursued a bad guy without his partner, or when a mom went searching for her child in a dangerous place all alone. I'm not victim blaming here. I'm reminding us that the place of rest is also a place of wisdom. We do not do life alone.

Third, Jonathan was rooted and grounded in faith. He relied on what he knew of the character and nature of God, knowing it is not God's intention for them to be tormented by the enemy. As discussed in chapter 2, to rest is "to remain confident: trust." Living from rest is to possess unwavering faith in God.

> *"Jonathan said, 'See now, we are going to cross over to the [Philistine] men and reveal ourselves to them. If they say*

to us, "Wait until we come to you," then we will stand in our place and not go up to them. But if they say, "Come up to us," we will go up, for the Lord has handed them over to us; and this shall be the sign to us.' When both of them revealed themselves to the garrison of the Philistines, the Philistines said, 'Look, the Hebrews are coming out of the holes where they have hidden themselves.' So the men of the garrison responded to Jonathan and his armor bearer, 'Come up to us and we will tell you something.' Jonathan said to his armor bearer, 'Climb up after me, for the Lord has given them into the hands of Israel.'

"Then Jonathan climbed up on his hands and feet, his armor bearer following after him. The enemy fell before Jonathan [in combat], and his armor bearer killed some of them after him." (1 Samuel 14:8-13 AMP)

Even though Jonathan's example of conducting himself from rest started with a knowing, as he walked, he sought confirmation for the next steps. He told his confidant his plan and his confidant affirmed the plan (1 Samuel 14:7). Like Gideon in Judges 6, Jonathan put a fleece before the Lord: If the enemy says, "Wait until we come to you," we do Plan A; if the enemy says, "Come up to us," then Plan B. Then, he stuck with the plan. Jonathan stepped out in faith, based on a knowing, and then confirmed what he felt God was speaking to him by trusting a confidant and putting a fleece before the Lord. This is living from a position of rest, and God met Jonathan where he was:

"So the Lord saved Israel that day, and the battle spread beyond Bethaven." (1 Samuel 14:23 AMP)

A FEW MORE EXAMPLES OF OPERATING FROM REST

Jonathan's story may remind you of David and Goliath from 1 Samuel 17, once again the Philistines were tormenting the Israelites.

> *"Then David spoke to the men who were standing by him, 'What will be done for the man who kills this Philistine and removes the disgrace [of his taunting] from Israel? For who is this uncircumcised Philistine that he has taunted and defied the armies of the living God?'"* (1 Samuel 17:26 AMP)

You see, David knew this gospel of rest. David had learned how to abide in the knowledge of God. His confident trust was in Jehovah Sabaoth, the LORD of hosts. (It is a title of JEHOVAH God's military might, His strength to fight and win battles.)[7] David didn't need additional information, and he didn't need anyone else's armor or equipment. He rested in the knowledge of God and acted from there.

> *"Then David said to the Philistine, 'You come to me with a sword, a spear, and a javelin, but I come to you in the name of the Lord of hosts, the God of the armies of Israel, whom you have taunted.'"* (1 Samuel 17:45 AMP)

David was attuned to the authority he accessed by the very name of God. He knew to operate from rest and not fret as he loosed heaven on earth.

Shadrach, Meshach, and Abednego are three more young men who knew how to rest in the knowledge of God. They too understood that the gospel of rest begins with "be still and know." The king had built a gigantic golden statue, 90' x 9', that he wanted the people to bow down and worship when the music played. But these boys refused, even though they were threatened with being thrown into the furnace.

> "*Shadrach, Meshach, and Abednego answered the king, 'O Nebuchadnezzar, we do not need to answer you on this point. If it be so, our God whom we serve is able to rescue us from the furnace of blazing fire, and He will rescue us from your hand, O king. But even if He does not, let it be known to you, O king, that we are not going to serve your gods or worship the golden image that you have set up!'*" (Daniel 3:16-18 AMP)

Even in the face of certain death, these men had unwavering confidence and complete trust in God. Whether God rescued them in this life or the next, they would not compromise. This is what it means to "be still and know." This is what it means to live from rest.

> "*The satraps, the prefects, the governors and the king's counselors gathered around them and saw that in regard to these men the fire had no effect on their bodies—their hair was not singed, their clothes were not scorched or damaged, even the smell of smoke was not on them.*
>
> "*Nebuchadnezzar responded and said, 'Blessed be the God of Shadrach, Meshach, and Abednego, who has sent His angel and rescued His servants who believed in, trusted in, and relied on Him! They violated the king's command and surrendered their bodies rather than serve or worship any god except their own God.'*" (Daniel 3:27-28 AMP)

Undaunted. This is what it looks like to have a garrison protecting the peace in your heart and mind, silencing the chaos.[3]

Daniel was another young man who knew what it was to remain steadfast. In Daniel chapter 6, King Darius, having not learned from King Nebuchadnezzar, established a royal statute and enforced an injunction that anyone who petitioned (prayed to) any god or man besides King Darius would be thrown into the den of lions. Yet, Daniel continued to pray to his God. And so, he was thrown into the lion's den. And yet, no injury whatsoever came of it. You see, even the king knew of Daniel's faith.

> *"Then the king was greatly pleased and ordered that Daniel be taken out of the den. So Daniel was taken out of the den, and no injury whatever was found on him, because he* **believed in and relied on and trusted in his God."** (Daniel 6:23 AMP)

In all of these examples, remaining steadfast and operating from rest was not just a characteristic of the person or people described, but also a testimony by which they and the observers came face to face with the knowledge of God. Remaining steadfast isn't just for your benefit. I love how the balance of Daniel 6 describes the aftermath:

> *"Then Darius the king wrote to all the peoples, nations, and speakers of every language who were living in all the land: 'May peace abound to you! I issue a decree that in all the dominion of my kingdom men are to [reverently] fear*

---

3. Philippians 4:7 in the Weymouth New Testament says: *"And the peace of God, which transcends all our powers of thought, will be a garrison to guard your hearts and minds in union with Christ Jesus."*

and tremble before the God of Daniel, for He is the living God, enduring and steadfast forever, and His kingdom is one which will not be destroyed, And His dominion will be forever.

He rescues and saves and performs signs and wonders In heaven and on earth—He who has rescued Daniel from the power of the lions.'

"So this [man] Daniel prospered and enjoyed success in the reign of Darius and in the reign of Cyrus the Persian." (Daniel 6:25-28 AMP)

We can see that abiding in the covenant of rest has the additional effect of influencing those around us for the sake of the kingdom.

If you want to learn how to be undaunted by what is seen and abide in the covenant of peace, invite the Holy Spirit to impart revelatory fortitude, to teach you and guide you, and unveil this supernatural reality. (See John 14:26; John 16:13; 1 Corinthians 2:10.)

Lord, help us to dwell in the secret place so that even when it seems like a tempest, we remain steadfast.

The examples of Jonathan, the Hebrew children, and Daniel are examples of staying grafted to the vine when others created chaos. The truth is, sometimes the unrest is of our own making. Sometimes, we lose our contentment with our current assignment that God has yet to graduate us from. Or maybe we think the season we're in is boring. Or we've graduated ourselves before we have learned all of the lessons that we needed to there. We fall out of rest because we want to slay giants without first tending sheep. We fall out of rest when we stray from our assignment and acquire responsibilities that were not meant for us. Sometimes we fall out of rest when we fail to complete the mission assigned.

In Leif Hetland's book, *Giant Slayers,* he explores the idea of seasons through the example of the life of David. He explains that David was uniquely situated to triumph over Goliath. The reason why others failed before David was that Goliath was David's God-given mission. Hetland takes it further and issued a challenge: "Problems exist that we are meant to solve. We may, in fact, be the only solution to some problems."

Ecclesiastes reminds us that for everything there is a season (Ecclesiastes 3:1). This season may be the giant slaying season, but if it's not, will you be faithful if it's the sheep tending season?

As we abide in Him, He reveals our assignment. When we faithfully show up for the assignment, HE IS WITH US! Grafted to the vine, habitually fixing our focus on Him, means we aren't distracted by assignments that weren't meant for us in the first place. A daily habit of faithfulness leads to a pattern of steadfastness and a lifestyle of rest as an operating system.

> "A DAILY HABIT OF FAITHFULNESS LEADS TO A PATTERN OF STEADFASTNESS AND A LIFESTYLE OF REST AS AN OPERATING SYSTEM."

EXPERIENCING THE STILLNESS AND KNOWING

My heart in writing this book is not only to expose you to a new paradigm, but to illustrate that God is doing this in me. It is an ongoing process, but it's too good to keep to myself. If He is doing this in me, He will do it in you, too. Abiding in rest is a journey. It's engaging a procedure of tweaks and adjustments to mindsets and behaviors as Holy Spirit reveals. Even though God was with me in supernatural ways through grief, loss, and tragedy,

I still have questions and grief still hurts. Even though God revealed to me His plan for me to abide in His rest, there are still moments of restlessness.

Rest is not the absence of emotion. It is the acknowledgment that our own strength does not hold us.

In the aftermath of all the grief and loss, there was a stillness. I can't specifically recall when the days stopped blurring together. Almost like when you make your routine drive to work for the millionth time and you get off at your exit and suddenly question how you got there. Somehow, you were lost in thought, muscle memory took over, and you just made it there on auto-pilot. This was kind of like that. I don't know how the kids were at school, dressed appropriately, or had sufficient lunches. It was a "one foot in front of the other" kind of a season. I just remember that the kids had returned to school, because the house was empty during the day.

It must have been early September. It was a school day and the children were at school. I was drained. It was as if my senses, which had been suppressed for an unknown period of time, suddenly returned to me. I felt like I was sitting under Elijah's tree from I Kings 19.

I wasn't praying that I would die. I was praying, "Why did my father die? Why did YOU not heal my father? Why did YOU allow all of this to happen?" I continued, "Angry with YOU doesn't begin to describe how I feel right now. I appreciate that You were with me. Thank You for not abandoning me, but why did Your presence not prevent death?! Thank You for Your presence, I guess, but why did You not heal any of them? I'M FRUSTRATED WITH YOU!"

Much to my surprise, I did not feel any thunder, scolding, rebuke, or discipline. Instead, it was as if I heard Him say, *"What else do you need to say to Me? What else do you want to say, my daughter?"*

And, as He did for Elijah, I, too, felt ministering angels. I, too, simply felt the urge to eat and drink and sleep and only do the next necessary thing. I, too, felt soothed and held as if His response was only, *"Rest, My child."*

This exchange lasted for days: me expressing anger, hurt, sadness, fear, frustration, and disbelief among other equally negative sentiments. Spirit of God conveying peace, understanding, and refuge.

Then one day, Lamentations 3 dropped in my heart.

> *"The thought of my suffering is bitter beyond words. I will never forget this awful time, as I grieve over my loss."*
> (Lamentations 3:19-20 NLT)

I decided it seemed fair enough to adopt Jeremiah's prayer as my own: "I'm never going to forget this, Lord. I'm never going to forget that You chose not to heal on this side of heaven! This is really painful. And if that one loss wasn't enough for my children to endure, YOU decided it would be best for them to lose all of this family at once. This really is an awful time. We are grieving over such tremendous losses."

Again, I didn't feel any rebuke whatsoever. I contacted one of my mentors, a pastor I have trusted for more than twenty-five years. I honestly expressed to him the sorrow and anger I felt.

His words ring in my ears to this day: "It's okay! Just don't build a house there."

That pastor probably doesn't know that his words were

life-giving. The validation that I could be mad and sad and not be outside of God's grace confirmed that I really was experiencing God and not just a selfish or earthly justification for my error. "Just don't build a house there." I knew that I wouldn't. I would allow myself this time to heal, but afterward, I knew that I would eventually take the next step.

For days, I prayed Lamentations 3:19-20. I had nothing else to say. And, in response, I continued to only feel the comfort of Heavenly Father: divine rest.

Then, one morning, it was as if Holy Spirit whispered to me, *"Do you think you can get to 'yet'?"* (You see, Lamentations 3:21 says, *"Yet, this I call to mind and therefore I have hope."* It's a portion of Scripture I have often turned to in my darkest hours. I am well familiar with the passage.) As if to interrupt, I felt myself blurt out, "I'm not at 'Great is Thy Faithfulness,' okay?! I'm just not there. Sorry!"

Again, I felt that still small voice. *"Just verse 21. Can you get to YET?"*

"Fine. Yes. 'Yet.' I still remember all of this crazy, stupid stuff I have had to go through, my family has had to go through, and I'm still mad about it. But yes, I can also say, 'Yet.'"

The next transition didn't take quite as long, maybe just two or three days. I would pray my loathing and I would also just whisper 'yet' at the end, as if to partner with hope.

Then one time, I just said aloud, "Yet this I call to mind and therefore I have hope."

Yes! I do, I have hope.

It was as if by saying it aloud, revelation knowledge flooded every cell of my body. I do not have to dwell on all of that sorrow. I can decide what I am going to call to mind. Today, I can choose to call to mind the faithfulness of God. I triumphantly declared in my spirit:

> "The faithful love of the Lord never ends! His mercies never cease. Great is his faithfulness; his mercies begin afresh each morning. I say to myself, 'The Lord is my inheritance; therefore, I will hope in him!'" (Lamentations 3:22-24 NLT)

In the same moments that I felt supernaturally reminded that HIS faithfulness does not depend on my circumstances, I also felt the Lord urging me to wrap up my time under this tree. In the same way that the angel told Elijah to get up and eat up for the journey ahead was long, I, too, felt that prompting: "Get up. Get ready. I am not done with you yet. I am preparing you for the next phase." I didn't feel scolded; I felt valued. I felt needed. I felt like my journey to date was not for nothing and would be used to serve a greater purpose. AND I felt invited to abide in this rest perpetually.

My new revelations of abiding rest do not prevent me from experiencing restlessness, but illuminate when I step out of rest. I recognize more quickly when I revert to relying on my strength. My seasons of distress or anxious thinking are shorter because I am quickened in my spirit to return to Him.

ACTIVATION

I invite you to consider a paradigm shift for your own life. I invite you to think about your part in sealing the covenant of peace. I suggest playing "Be Still" by Red Rocks Worship (Jake Espy, Tyler Roberts, and Adaeze Noelle Azubuike) for a more immersive activation.

I. Are you aware of the season that you are in and do you know what your assignment is in this season? Is there anything that you have assigned yourself to do that maybe isn't your job? Are you waiting when you should be going? Or going when you ought to be waiting?

Let's ask Holy Spirit:

> *Holy Spirit, thank You for confirming in my spirit what season I am in and the assignment that I have in this season. Please reveal to me any area where I am straying from my assignment.*

Record what Holy Spirit reveals.

_____

_____

_____

_____

_____

_____

2. Does the Great I AM hold His rightful place in your life or have you relegated Him to a limited role?

Let's ask Holy Spirit:

Holy Spirit, thank You for revealing to me the areas of my life in which I have failed to acknowledge Your Lordship.

Record what Holy Spirit reveals.

_____

_____

_____

_____

_____

_____

3. Do you believe in, rely on, and trust in God? Are you firm, confident, and undismayed?

Let's ask Holy Spirit:

Holy Spirit, thank You for revealing to me the areas of my life in which I have failed to wholly rely on You. Thank You for revealing areas where I lack confidence in You or have become dismayed.

Record what Holy Spirit reveals.

_____

_____

_____

_____

_____

_____

In your own words, pray this prayer:

> *Lord, help me be like King Jehoshaphat and consecrate time to hear from You. Help me to keep my eyes on You and acknowledge the moments when I do not know what to do. Teach me to abide in You so that I can have faith sufficient to move when You move. I partner with John 16:13 and invite You, Spirit of Truth, to reveal to me who You want to be in my life at this moment. Reveal to me how You see me in this moment. Thank You for enabling me to hear and recognize Your voice (John 10:4).*

Write down whatever comes to mind.

_____

_____

_____

_____

_____

_____

_____

_____

_____

_____

_____

_____

_____

_____

_____

_____

_____

_____

CHAPTER 5

KNOW GOD

THE SECOND PART of Psalm 46:10 is, "and know that I am God." "And know" denotes the ability to recognize the character of Yahweh He is trying to specifically reveal in this season. In every season, He is Savior, Redeemer, and Lord. In some seasons, He is revealing Himself as Jehovah-Rohi, in others Jehovah El Roi, in others Jehovah Jireh. You see, He is the Great I AM. That means He is exactly what and who you need when needed. We must know who He is to abide in rest.

"When Jesus arrived in the villages of Caesarea Philippi, he asked his disciples, 'What are people saying about who the Son of Man is?' They replied, 'Some think he is John the Baptizer, some say Elijah, some Jeremiah or one of the other prophets.' He pressed them, 'And how about you? Who do you say I am?' Simon Peter said, 'You're the Christ, the Messiah, the Son of the living God.' Jesus came

back, 'God bless you, Simon, son of Jonah! You didn't get that answer out of books or from teachers. My Father in heaven, God himself, let you in on this secret of who I really am. And now I'm going to tell you who you are, really are. You are Peter, a rock. This is the rock on which I will put together my church, a church so expansive with energy that not even the gates of hell will be able to keep it out.'"
(Matthew 16:13-18 MSG)

When Peter conveyed that he knew who Jesus was, Jesus revealed Peter's identity. I believe Jesus' question is asking, "How have YOU defined Me? How have you limited Me? What box have you put Me in?" Because, you see, in Exodus chapter 3, God defined Himself... as LIMITLESS.

"But Moses protested, 'If I go to the people of Israel and tell them, "The God of your ancestors has sent me to you," they will ask me, "What is his name?" Then what should I tell them?' God replied to Moses, 'I Am Who I Am. Say this to the people of Israel: I Am has sent me to you.' God also said to Moses, 'Say this to the people of Israel: Yahweh, the God of your ancestors—the God of Abraham, the God of Isaac, and the God of Jacob—has sent me to you. This is my eternal name, my name to remember for all generations.'"
(Exodus 3:13-15 NLT)

What God meant was HE IS THE ONE who is all things to all people. Whatever they may need in the moment, HE WAS that before they got to the moment. For example:

For Hagar, He was the God who hears and sees: **Jehovah El Roi.**

"And the angel also said, 'You are now pregnant and will give birth to a son. You are to name him Ishmael (which means "God hears"), for the Lord has heard your cry of distress...' Thereafter, Hagar used another name to refer to the Lord, who had spoken to her. She said, 'You are the God who sees me.' She also said, 'Have I truly seen the One who sees me?' So that well was named Beer-lahai-roi (which means 'well of the Living One who sees me'). It can still be found between Kadesh and Bered." (Genesis 16:11, 13-14 NLT)

Remember, Hagar was the servant of Abraham and Sarah. After God promised Abraham descendants, the couple was discouraged about how long it took for God's promise to be fulfilled. So ultimately, Sarah took matters into her own hands and thought she could use Hagar as a surrogate. While her plan worked, it became disconcerting. Sarah began to feel contempt toward Hagar.

I interpret Genesis 16:1-6 to reveal a mutual hostility between the women leading to Hagar leaving the group and going out alone. I can only imagine how isolated, alone, and abandoned she felt. And yet, we read how God had compassion on her. He came to her, revealing Himself to her in her despair. She was seen.

For David, He was **Shepherd**: *"The Lord is my shepherd; I have all that I need"* (Psalm 23:1 NLT).

David was a shepherd as a boy. He tended his father's flock. In fact, that is what he was doing right before he carried sandwiches to his brothers when Goliath was tormenting the Israelites. It was in those pastures with his father's sheep that he learned to play the harp. That harp is what gave him an opportunity to spend time in the presence of King Saul. He played his harp to soothe King Saul when King Saul was tormented in his spirit.

While many of David's stories are contained within the psalms, I'm sure there are countless more about how David experienced God as his Shepherd. In the same way David cared for the sheep, I'm certain that he identified as a sheep in God's pasture, being led beside still waters, guided and corrected, and followed by goodness and mercy. There's no disputing that the favor of God rested on David. Even though he made many mistakes, he was broken and contrite before the Lord. He experienced the care of the Good Shepherd and left us the anecdotes so that we, too, may experience the Lord as our Shepherd.

For Moses, He was what he needed in the moment. According to Exodus 17:8–16, He was **Jehovah Nissi**, the Lord is my banner.

> *"Then Amalek [and his people] came and fought with Israel at Rephidim. So Moses said to Joshua, 'Choose men for us and go out, fight against Amalek [and his people]. Tomorrow I will stand on the top of the hill with the staff of God in my hand.' So Joshua did as Moses said, and fought with Amalek; and Moses, Aaron, and Hur went up to the hilltop. Now when Moses held up his hand, Israel prevailed, and when he lowered his hand [due to fatigue], Amalek prevailed. But Moses' hands were heavy and he grew tired. So they took a stone and put it under him, and he sat on it. Then Aaron and Hur held up his hands, one on one side and one on the other side; so it was that his hands were steady until the sun set. So Joshua overwhelmed and*

defeated Amalek and his people with the edge of the sword. Then the Lord said to Moses, 'Write this in the book as a memorial and recite it to Joshua, that I will utterly wipe out the memory of Amalek [and his people] from under heaven.' And Moses built an altar and named it The Lord Is My Banner; saying, 'The Lord has sworn [an oath]; the Lord will have war against [the people of] Amalek from generation to generation.'" (Exodus 17:8–16 AMP)

Merriam-Webster defines *banner* as:

"A piece of cloth attached by one edge to a staff and used by a leader (such as a monarch or feudal lord) as a standard."

"A conspicuous object (such as a banner) formerly carried at the top of a pole and used to mark a rallying point especially in battle or to serve as an emblem."

"A name, slogan, or goal associated with a particular group or ideology."

Moses' identity in Yahweh is affirmed when the Lord is Moses' banner. The ideology of Yahweh is embraced. Moses' association with Yahweh is acknowledged. It is a recognition that Israel prevailed only because of Yahweh's intervention. I believe this illustration of the Lord as our banner is what Paul meant when he wrote Philippians 2:13 (AMP):

"For it is [not your strength, but it is] God who is effectively at work in you, both to will and to work [that is, strengthening, energizing, and creating in you the longing and the ability to fulfill your purpose] for His good pleasure."

Moses models acknowledging and confessing his total reliance on the Lord. He knew that in the same way Spirit of God hovered over the waters, he now needed Spirit of God to hover over this situation.

Moses offers us many examples of the different revelations of God. When the water at Marah was bitter, He was **Jehovah Rapha.**

> *"He said, 'If you will listen carefully to the voice of the Lord your God and do what is right in his sight, obeying his commands and keeping all his decrees, then I will not make you suffer any of the diseases I sent on the Egyptians; for I am the Lord who heals you.'"* (Exodus 15:26 NLT)

This is important. God reveals Himself to us in different seasons and different ways. At Marah, they didn't need Jehovah Nissi. What if they had left God in the box of banner? They would have missed that He is I AM, and at Marah, He was I AM HEALER. What He was for you yesterday might not be what you need Him to be today, and if you are living in the miracle from yesterday, you might be missing the miracle He wants to give you today.

In Hagar's moment, she didn't need David's Shepherd or Moses' Banner. She needed to be seen. She needed to KNOW GOD SAW HER. She needed to know He was aware of her. On the other hand, Moses didn't need to just be seen by God; he needed a banner, he needed God to hover over the battle for the victory. If we expect God to only be for us what He is for our neighbor, we may miss who God wants to be for us in our moment. Remember, He is I AM. He knows what you need before you need it and He has already made a way before you got there. If you restrict His definition to that which He was for your friend, you're not letting Him be all He wants for you.

Another revelation of God to Moses was as **Jehovah Machsi**, the Lord is my Refuge (Psalm 91:9).

We can read all about Moses in the book of Exodus. His story is replete with the need for God as his Refuge. From the tiny baby in a basket, the teenage fugitive hiding in the wilderness, the encounters with Pharoah, and the plight of the complaining Israelites wandering in desert, Moses can tell us firsthand what it is like to know God as a Refuge.

For the Israelites in Egypt, he was **Jehovah Mephalti**, the Lord my Deliverer.

For the Israelites, God was a great many things, but a main character was deliverer. God used Moses and miraculously delivered the Israelites from Egypt. He doesn't get that name just because of the ten plagues; the Deliverer parted seas, drowned the Israelites' enemies, delivered them from famine, and delivered them from their idolatry.

Maybe you or someone you hold dear are addicted to drugs or alcohol or pornography or the internet or social media, or maybe you find yourself in another form of bondage and you need the Deliverer. He IS (Exodus 3:7-8).

For Jeremiah, he was **Jehovah Tsidkenu**, the Lord our righteousness (Jeremiah 23:6 and 33:16).

You see, God anointed Jeremiah as a prophet to the nations. The unfortunate reality was, much like the times we find ourselves in now, righteous living, uprightness was pretty unpopular. In Jeremiah's time, there was so much unrighteousness all around him. It was depressing. He bemoaned all about it in the book of Lamentations. Jeremiah needed the revelation of God as Righteousness, the compass, his plumbline, the ultimate impermeable standard by which to measure the listeners.

For Ezekiel, God was revealed as **Jehovah Shammah**, meaning "Jehovah is there," the name given to the city in Ezekiel's vision in Ezekiel 48:35.

Ezekiel, Jeremiah, and Daniel were contemporaries, all called by God to preach a message of repentance and implore the people, to whom they were sent, to return to right relationship with God. In a time when unholiness was common, God revealed Himself to Ezekiel as One who had not abandoned him, but was in fact with him. Many of Ezekiel's visions pay homage to a God who desired to be among His people.

Recall the vision of the dry bones while it seemed all hope was lost and all that remained was a valley of dry bones, people dead in their sin. God revealed to Ezekiel that all was not lost, that Ezekiel could prophesy life and breath back into those "bones." God is here. It is by Him and through Him that we have the victory even in what may seem like hopeless situations.

For Gideon, God revealed Himself as **Jehovah Shalom**, the Lord is our peace.

Oh, Gideon. There's so much to say about Gideon. This was the guy that was hiding in the wine cellar threshing wheat when the Spirit of the Lord came to him and called him a mighty warrior. Of course, he was confused because he knew he was hiding. He certainly didn't identify as a warrior much less a mighty one. God provided Gideon with a source of courage, strength, and peace even though the odds were stacked against him.

"So Gideon built an altar there to the Lord, and called it

The-Lord-Is-Peace. To this day it is still in Ophrah of the Abiezrites." (Judges 6:24 NKJV)

Maybe you, like Gideon, feel the odds are stacked against you and you are not qualified for the role you were assigned. The character of Jehovah Shalom shows up on the scene and gives you that inner peace, rest, confidence, and assurance you need to remain steadfast.

For Abraham, in Genesis 17, He was **Jehovah El Shaddai**, God Almighty.

"When Abram was ninety-nine years old, the Lord appeared to him and said, 'I am God Almighty; Walk [habitually] before Me [with integrity, knowing that you are always in My presence], and be blameless and complete [in obedience to Me].'" (Genesis 17:1 AMP)

We all need that reminder, don't we? We need to experience the Lord as Jehovah El Shaddai, God Almighty. We must be reminded to keep the habit of walking out our lives with integrity. We operate with the knowledge there is no where we can go that God is not already there.

Like for Moses, God revealed Himself in multiple ways to Abraham. In Genesis 22:14, He was **Jehovah Jireh.** He provided the ram in the bush.

How many of us have been called by God to undertake difficult tasks? Isn't it amazing He doesn't ask us to do anything or go anywhere that He has not already prepared? Maybe it was because Abraham was God's friend he did not fret, or maybe it was because Abraham trusted God unswervingly that he was considered God's friend. Either way, Abraham already knew

God was Jireh before he set out with his son. Consider verse 5, where Abraham told his servants, *"We will come back to you."* Even though he knew God asked him to sacrifice his dream, lineage, and legacy on the altar, he also knew it was test. He also expected God to provide.

Lord, help me to have faith like Abraham and KNOW You as provider even before the test.

For Mary, He was **Jehovah Emmanuel**, God with us (see Matthew 1:23 and John 1:14).

Mary is my hero in so many ways. When the angel Gabriel appeared to Mary to tell her she would bear a son, Mary could have responded in so many ways. While she was confused and had questions, her response was simple: *"May it be so"* (Luke 1:38).

Luke reported the words of the angel: *"Greetings, you who are highly favored! The Lord is with you"* (Luke 1:28 NIV). Isn't it fitting, then, that was also the name she was to give her Son: Emmanuel?

David reminds us in the 139th Psalm that God is ALWAYS with us, there is no where we can go to escape His presence. If you're reading this now and you are not feeling or sensing the nearness of the Shepherd, read Psalm 139 and invite Holy Spirit to reveal the presence and nearness of our loving Father.

In Isaiah 49:26 and 60:16, He was **Jehovah-Go'el**, The Lord My Redeemer.

After war and sin wreaked havoc on Israel, God used Isaiah to declare that God doesn't leave things awry. He is the Great Redeemer and He will restore.

If you feel like you are a victim of injustice or have felt robbed of victories you could almost taste, allow Holy Spirit to reveal to you Jehovah Go'el, the Great Redeemer. I stand with you and declare Isaiah 49, Isaiah 60, and Joel 2 over your life and the lives of your family. He will redeem and restore, and then He will pour out His Spirit upon you, equipping you for what lies ahead. As the song writer said, "If it's not good, He's not done." (See also Romans 8:28-29.)

I would be remiss to omit the first characterization of God we find in the biblical record: **Jehovah-Bara**, the Lord the Creator (see Genesis 1:1; Isaiah 40:28; Psalm 104; Job 38-42). Psalm 139, Jeremiah 1, and Isaiah 49 are additional reminders of God the Creator.

You—yes, you my friend—were created, fashioned intentionally by a Creator with divine plans and purposes for your life. You are blessed and highly favored and God is *with* YOU.

As you journey with me in these next few chapters, I invite you to partner with your God-given identity. You were made on purpose! You are no accident! You are not a mishap. God did not cobble together all the leftover pieces and make you as an afterthought. You were made in the very image and likeness of God Himself (Genesis 1:27) and He invites you to partner with Him as you continue to learn how to *rest* in Him.

Maybe as we're sitting here, you can think of many more characteristics, different names, identities, attributes that God represented for people in the Bible or even for you, but it all comes back to "I AM."

God did not change. He does not change.

"Jesus Christ is the same yesterday and today and forever."
(Hebrews 13:8 NIV)

"For I am the Lord, I do not change [but remain faithful to My covenant with you]; that is why you, O sons of Jacob, have not come to an end." (Malachi 3:6 AMP)

"Every good thing given and every perfect gift is from above; it comes down from the Father of lights [the Creator and Sustainer of the heavens], in whom there is no variation [no rising or setting] or shadow cast by His turning [for He is perfect and never changes]." (James 1:17 AMP)

We change. Our circumstances change. The way we need God changes, and in every season, there is an opportunity for God to reveal more of Himself to us.

I preached about peace that passes understanding, but until I needed that kind of peace, I didn't realize that what I knew was the Scripture and not Jehovah Shalom. When I was weary from caring for Gram and was looking forward to going home to rest, grieve, and recuperate, only to realize that the true storm had just begun, God revealed Himself as Jehovah Shalom.

I taught plenty about the 23rd Psalm, but it wasn't until I experienced a complete reliance on His leading, His guidance, and His manifest presence that I realized I had known the psalm and not Jehovah-Rohi. In the aftermath of massive grief from all the losses of dear family, I was incapable, in my strength, of navigating all of the normal life stuff. It wasn't like a meet and greet; it wasn't like I was sitting on the side of my bed and God introduced Himself as my Shepherd. Instead, I woke up one day with this divine realization that THIS is what the 23rd Psalm means. This experience of God enabling me to put one foot in front of the other one, this is THE LORD IS MY SHEPHERD!

And THAT is the mystery. God reveals Himself to us at the exact right time. He knows what we need and when we need it. The mystery is, He IS I AM.

- *"He said to them, 'The privilege of intimately knowing the mystery of God's kingdom realm has been granted to you, but not to the others, where everything is revealed in parables.'"* (Mark 4:11 TPT)

- *"I give all my praises and glory to the one who has more than enough power to make you strong and keep you steadfast through the promises found in my gospel; that is, the proclamation of Jesus, the Anointed One. This wonderful news includes the unveiling of the mystery kept secret from the dawn of creation until now."* (Romans 16:25 TPT)

- *"For this wonderful mystery, which I briefly described, was given to me by divine revelation, so that whenever you read it you will be able to understand my revelation and insight into the secret mystery of the Messiah. There has never been a generation that has been given the detailed understanding of this glorious and divine mystery until now. He kept it a secret until this generation. God is revealing it only now to his sacred apostles and prophets by the Holy Spirit. Here's the secret: The gospel of grace has made you, non-Jewish believers, into coheirs of his promise through your union with him.*

    And you have now become members of his body—one with the Anointed One! I have been made a messenger of this wonderful news by the gift of grace that works through me. Even though I am the least significant of all his holy believ-

ers, this grace-gift was imparted when the manifestation of
his power came upon me. Grace alone empowers me so that
I can boldly preach this wonderful message to non-Jewish
people, sharing with them the unfading, inexhaustible riches
of Christ, which are beyond comprehension. My passion is to
enlighten every person to this divine mystery. It was hidden
for ages past until now, and kept a secret in the heart of God,
the Creator of all." (Ephesians 3:3-9 TPT)

- "I am contending for you that your hearts will be wrapped
  in the comfort of heaven and woven together into love's fab-
  ric. This will give you access to all the riches of God as you
  experience the revelation of God's great mystery—Christ.
  For our spiritual wealth is in him, like hidden treasure waiting to be discovered—heaven's wisdom and endless riches of
  revelation knowledge." (Colossians 2:2-3 TPT)

- "Look with wonder at the depth of the Father's marvelous
  love that he has lavished on us! He has called us and made us
  his very own beloved children. The reason the world doesn't
  recognize who we are is that they didn't recognize him." (1
  John 3:1 TPT)

When we truly understand that the whole character of God
is both unfathomable and completely sufficient, our only
response is rest.

God is everything that we need, in every season and every situation. We can rest because of who He is. When we are confident
in Him, when we trust Him as I AM _____.
(Fill in the blank with whatever you need today. Maybe you
need God to hover over your situation. Maybe you need heal-

ing, provision, restoration, or something else. Whatever it is, allow the Holy Spirit to enable you to trust the God WHO IS.)

We rest assured that He has everything under control. If He has

"WHEN WE TRULY UNDERSTAND THAT THE WHOLE CHARACTER OF GOD IS BOTH UNFATHOMABLE AND COMPLETELY SUFFICIENT, OUR ONLY RESPONSE IS REST."

everything under control, the only natural result is we can rest, we can be at peace. We claim the promise in 2 Peter 1:3 (AMP):

"For His divine power has bestowed on us [absolutely] everything necessary for [a dynamic spiritual] life and godliness, through true and personal knowledge of Him who called us by His own glory and excellence."

ACTIVATION

Before you get started with this activation, I recommend listening to "I AM" by Eddie James and "Live Up to Your Name" by Danny Gokey.

Take out your journal and record the answers to the following questions:

1. Holy Spirit, how do You want to reveal Yourself to me in this season? What character of Yourself are You trying to make known to me?

_____

_____

_____

_____

_____

_____

2. In what ways are You making Yourself known to me?

_____

_____

_____

_____

_____

_____

3. What can I do, how can I align my thoughts, or what steps can I take to recognize You in my life?

_____

_____

_____

_____

_____

_____

_____

_____

_____

_____

_____

_____

_____

_____

_____

_____

_____

_____

_____

_____

_____

_____

_____

_____

CHAPTER 6

KNOW YOURSELF

HOW WOULD YOU talk, walk, think, and conduct yourself differently if you were heir to the throne? If you were a prince or princess, how would conduct yourself? If your daddy was the king, and you were THE heir to his throne, how would your perspective of yourself be different than it is right now?

Well, guess WHAT? You are an heir to the kingdom. The Bible says we are co-heirs with Christ:

- *"Thus we have been set free to experience our **rightful heritage.** You can tell for sure that you are now fully adopted as his own children because God sent the Spirit of his Son into our lives crying out, 'Papa! Father!' Doesn't that privilege of intimate conversation with God make it plain that you are not a slave, but a child? And if **you are a child, you're also** *an heir, with complete access to the inheritance."* (Galatians 4:6-7 MSG)

- "Therefore you are no longer a slave (bond-servant), but a son; and if a son, **then also an heir** through [the gracious act of] God [through Christ]." (Galatians 4:7 AMP)

- "Now we're no longer living like slaves under the law, but we enjoy being God's very own sons and daughters! And because we're his, **we can access everything our Father has**—for we are **heirs** because of what God has done!" (Galatians 4:7 TPT)

- "The Spirit Himself testifies and confirms together with our spirit [assuring us] that we [believers] are children of God. And if [we are His] children, **[then we are His] heirs also: heirs of God and fellow heirs with Christ [sharing His spiritual blessing and inheritance]**, if indeed we share in His suffering so that we may also share in His glory." (Romans 8:16-17 AMP)

- "For you [who are born-again have been reborn from above—spiritually transformed, renewed, sanctified and] are all children of God **[set apart for His purpose with full rights and privileges]** through faith in Christ Jesus. For all of you who were baptized into Christ [into a spiritual union with the Christ, the Anointed] have clothed yourselves with Christ [that is, you have taken on His characteristics and values]. There is [now no distinction in regard to salvation] neither Jew nor Greek, there is neither slave nor free, there is neither male nor female; for you [who believe]Are all one in Christ Jesus [no one can claim a spiritual superiority]. **And if** *you belong to Christ [if you are in Him], then you are Abraham's descendants, and [spiritual] heirs according to [God's] promise.*" (Galatians 3:26-29 AMP)

- "*He predestined and lovingly planned for us to be **adopted to Himself as [His own] children** through Jesus Christ, in accordance with the kind intention and good pleasure of His will.... In Him also we have received an **inheritance [a destiny—we were claimed by God as His own]**, having been **predestined (chosen, appointed beforehand)** according to the purpose of Him who works everything in agreement with the counsel and design of His will[.]*" (Ephesians 1:5, 11 AMP)

- "*But when [in God's plan] the proper time had fully come, God sent His Son, born of a woman, born under the [regulations of the] Law, so that He might redeem and liberate those who were under the Law, that we [who believe] might be adopted as sons [**as God's children with all rights as fully grown members of a family**].*" (Galatians 4:4-5 AMP)

- "*But you are God's chosen treasure—priests who are kings, a spiritual 'nation' **set apart as God's devoted ones**. He called you out of darkness to experience his marvelous light, and now **he claims you as his very own**. He did this so that you would broadcast his glorious wonders throughout the world.*" (1 Peter 2:9 AMP)

This is the GOOD news. We are not orphans, slaves, or sinners.

We have been adopted and chosen. We are the holy priesthood. We are CO-HEIRS! Sometimes, we have identified ourselves differently from the way God has identified us. Sometimes, that identity limits our potential. What if we identified ourselves as God identifies us?

WHAT IS YOUR IDENTITY IN CHRIST?

You may consider the verses above theoretical or lofty ideas about our identity in Christ. Let's consider some practical examples of the difference between God-given identity and the limiting beliefs we adopt as our identity.

David shows us that our identity is not limited by our self-image or the identity put on us by our family.

David identified himself as meaningless, less than, merely a shepherd.

> *"'Who am I, and what is my family in Israel that I should be the king's son-in-law?' David exclaimed. 'My father's family is nothing!'"* (1 Samuel 18:18 NLT)

> *"When Saul's men said these things to David, he replied, 'How can a poor man from a humble family afford the bride price for the daughter of a king?'"* (1 Samuel 18:23 NLT)

But God saw him as LEADER.

> *"One of the servants said to Saul, 'One of Jesse's sons from Bethlehem is a talented harp player. Not only that—he is **a brave warrior, a man of war, and has good judgment. He is also a fine-looking young man, and the Lord is with him.**'"* (1 Samuel 16:18 NLT)

> *"David continued to succeed in everything he did, for the Lord was with him."* (1 Samuel 18:14 NLT)

"Now go and say to my servant David, 'This is what the Lord of Heaven's Armies has declared: I took you from tending sheep in the pasture and selected you to be the leader of my people Israel.'" (2 Samuel 7:8 NLT)

Moses shows us that our identity is not limited by our weaknesses. Moses identified himself as stutterer, stammerer, unable to lead.

"Moses raised another objection to God: 'Master, please, I don't talk well. I've never been good with words, neither before nor after you spoke to me. I stutter and stammer...' He said, 'Oh, Master, please! Send somebody else!'" (Exodus 4:10, 13 MSG)

But God identified him as called, sent, leader, and deliverer. (See Exodus 3:10-22; 4:12, 15-17)

Hagar's story proves that our identity is not limited to how people view us. Hagar identified herself as outcast, excluded, runaway, hidden, humiliated (see Genesis 16:7).

But God SAW HER with understanding and compassion.

"And He said, 'Hagar, Sarai's maid, where did you come from and where are you going?' And she said, 'I am running away from my mistress Sarai.' Then the Angel of the Lord said to her, 'I will greatly multiply your descendants so that they will be too many to count.' The Angel of the Lord continued, 'Behold, you are with child, And you will bear a son; And you shall name him Ishmael (God hears), Because the Lord has heard and paid attention to your persecution (suffering).'" (Genesis 16:8, 10-11 AMP)

*"Then she called the name of the Lord who spoke to her,
'You are God Who Sees'; for she said, 'Have I not even here
[in the wilderness] remained alive after seeing Him [who
sees me with understanding and compassion]?'"* (Genesis
16:13 AMP)

**Jeremiah reassures us that our identity is not limited by
our insecurities.**

Jeremiah identified himself as incapable and too young. But
God identified him as SET APART, PROPHET TO NATIONS.

*"'I knew you before I formed you in your mother's womb.
Before you were born I set you apart and appointed you as
my prophet to the nations.' 'O Sovereign Lord,' I said, 'I can't
speak for you! I'm too young!' The Lord replied, 'Don't say,
"I'm too young," for you must go wherever I send you and
say whatever I tell you.'"* (Jeremiah 1:5-7 NLT)

**Saul/Paul of Tarsus demonstrates that our identity is not
limited by our past.**

Sometimes people identify us and limit our potential. In
Acts 9:13, Saul is a terrible persecutor of the churches, But God,
in Acts 9:15, identified him as a special messenger. We know that
Paul wrote half of the New Testament!

**Jacob, who became Israel, shows us that our identity is
not limited by our actions.**

In Genesis 32:28, Jacob was identified as cheater and sup-
planter, but God renamed him Israel: GOD PREVAILS.

**Abram became Abraham, revealing that our identity is
not limited by human or earthly definitions.** You see, Abram

means limited/defined, but Abraham means limitless.

> *"No longer shall your name be Abram (exalted father), But your name shall be Abraham (father of a multitude); For I will make you the father of many nations."* (Genesis 17:5 AMP)

Simon Peter shows us that our identity is not limited to our profession. In Matthew 4:18, he was transformed from fisherman to fisher of men.

> *"And I say to you that you are Peter, and on this rock I will build My church; and the gates of Hades (death) will not overpower it [by preventing the resurrection of the Christ]."* (Matthew 16:18 AMP)

Gideon's story is an illustration that our identity is not limited by our status.

Gideon identified himself as insignificant (Judges 6:15), but God saw him as a mighty warrior (Judges 6:12).

Mary offers an example that our identity is not limited to what has been. Mary went from being a lowly servant girl to blessed and highly favored. And the reason Mary is my hero is that she adopted for herself God's identity.

> *"For he set his tender gaze upon me, his lowly servant girl. And from here on, everyone will know that I have been favored and blessed."* (Luke 1:48 TPT)

Some of us have had seasons, or maybe are in one right now, where we identify as our predicament, but God sees our potential.

1. Elijah identified himself as spent, weary, done, down and out, depressed, but God still saw him as sent, chosen, and called (1 Kings 19).

2. Mary Magdalene identified as demon-possessed, but God saw her as a disciple of Jesus, missionary even (Luke 8, Acts 1).

3. The Samaritan woman at the well identified as adulterer. But God saw her as appointed. Some say she was the first missionary (John 4).

4. For the adulterous woman from John 8, THEY identified her as accused, but Jesus saw her as ATONED, absolved.

In this season, God has been unveiling the layers of my God-given identity. Simultaneously, He has been revealing Himself in deeper, more profound ways.

During our COVID adventures, as my daughter referred to them, God showed me He called me to be a mother to my children. My primary role was not provider, it was mother, to nurture and mentor, to love and cherish. Simultaneously, He revealed Himself as friend and companion. Truly, He was with us. We felt His presence throughout our playing, traveling, and being a family.

When we moved to Kansas, He reminded me that He called me to be a wife and helpmate to my husband. My identity wasn't rooted in my profession. Instead, my family was a calling unto itself.

At the same time, He showed us He is Shepherd. It was, and still is, like an illustrated sermon, complete with sheep, lambs, green pastures, still waters, and shepherd's crooks. John 10 and

Psalm 23 have become so real, even my children take every opportunity to photograph, paint, preach, and sing about the Lord
our Shepherd.

Through illness and injury with my children, God saw me
as steadfast, even when I saw myself overwhelmed and fretful.
During their respective journeys to health, God refined me,
slowly uncovering a steadfastness. He taught me how to keep
praying and trusting, even when the answers didn't manifest as
quickly as we hoped. Through these experiences, He revealed
Himself as Sovereign. I encountered the God of Job in a way
I didn't think possible. He didn't answer when I thought He
should. Yet, He sustained me in the meanwhile, demonstrating
His character of sufficient grace.

Because I knew him as Sovereign and experienced His sufficient and sustaining grace with my children, I was prepared to
trust Him when it came to my grandmother and my father.

He used one season to prepare me for the next one. He revealed His character and nature that I would need to lean into.
And He cultivated skills and characteristics in me which were
essential. My prayer for you is that you will have spiritual eyes
to see the fingerprints of God on your life. I pray you will recognize that the previous seasons have qualified you for the one
you're in and have yet to face.

ACTIVATION

To enhance your experience, I recommend listening to "New Name Written Down in Glory" by Charity Gayle.

Imagine yourself as heir to an earthly throne, royalty, crowned prince or princess. Maybe you envision yourself as the daughter or son of the king, or a crowned prince of Saudi Arabia or the Woman King from the recent blockbuster. Take out your journal and sit quietly for a few moments. Write down whatever comes to mind in response to the questions below, or use the space provided:

1. What thoughts do you think about yourself that you wouldn't think anymore? How would you view yourself differently?

_____

_____

_____

_____

_____

_____

2. What are some things that you say which maybe don't belong in the mouth of royalty?

_____

_____

_____

_____

_____

_____

3. What could it look like then, it you embraced and partnered with your true identity as co-heir with Christ?

_____

_____

_____

_____

_____

_____

Now, as we move to a posture of prayer, let's invite a conversation with the Lord. Let's ask Him what His answers are to the questions:

1. Holy Spirit, how do You see me? What do You love about me?

_____

_____

_____

_____

_____

_____

2. In what ways are You drawing out the identity You see in me?

_____

_____

_____

_____

_____

3. What can I do, how can I align my thoughts, or what steps can I take to recognize how You see me?

_____

_____

_____

_____

_____

_____

_____

_____

_____

_____

_____

_____

_____

_____

_____

_____

_____

_____

_____

_____

_____

_____

_____

_____

CHAPTER 7

LEARN TO ABIDE

TURN WITH ME to John 15:5-11, the picture painted by The Message Bible is a great illustration:

*"I am the Vine, you are the branches. **When you're joined with me and I with you, the relation intimate and organic, the harvest is sure to be abundant.** Separated, you can't produce a thing. Anyone who separates from me is deadwood, gathered up and thrown on the bonfire. **But if you make yourselves at home with me and my words are at home in you, you can be sure that whatever you ask will be listened to and acted upon.** This is how my Father shows who he is—when you produce grapes, when you mature as my disciples.*

*"**I've loved you the way my Father has loved me. Make yourselves at home in my love. If you keep my commands, you'll remain intimately at home in my love.***

That's what I've done—kept my Father's commands and made myself at home in his love.

"I've told you these things for a purpose: that my joy might be your joy, and your joy wholly mature."

Jesus is saying that when we abide in Him and have intimacy and organic relationship with Him, we can produce a guaranteed harvest. Plus, if we remain in union with Him, whatever we ask "will be listened to and acted upon." And that's not all. If we abide in Him, our *"joy may be made full* and *complete* and *overflowing"* (John 15:11 AMP). With full, complete, and overflowing joy, we will most definitely be at rest.

So, let's reiterate: if we create a habitation, a resting place for Him, we will have the mind of Christ, and since we have the mind of Christ, we ask for or desire things in accordance with His desires. When our desires are in one accord with Him, we "may ask for anything [we] want, and it will be granted." He explains that this is possible by allowing His words to be at home in us.

How can we abide in Christ? We have to be intimately familiar with Him. How can we be intimately familiar with Him? We know the Word (Proverbs 2; Colossians 3:16). We read the Bible (Psalm 119), we memorize it (2 Timothy 3:15), we hide His Word in our hearts (Psalm 119:11); we meditate on it day and night (Joshua 1:8; Psalm 1:2). We recognize that what Paul wrote to the church in Rome is true for us today:

"Even if it was written in Scripture long ago, you can be sure it's written for us. God wants the combination of His steady, constant calling and warm, personal counsel in Scripture to come to characterize us, keeping us alert for whatever He will do next." (Romans 15:4 MSG)

Let's also look at what Jesus said in John 16:33 (AMP):

"I have told you these things, so that in Me you may have [perfect] peace. In the world you have tribulation and distress and suffering, **but be courageous [be confident, be undaunted, be filled with joy];** *I have overcome the world. [My conquest is accomplished,* **My victory abiding.***]"*

In present tense, He said, "IN ME you may have rest." How can we be like Jesus and be "undaunted" by chaos or confusion around us? (Remember chapter 3, when Jesus was asleep in a crazy storm.) In Him, we can have perfect peace. Grafted to the vine, we can be courageous, confident, and undaunted. This is a "right now" promise. This is the covenant of peace. When we do our part to cultivate an intimate relationship with Him we invoke the covenant of peace.

James takes on this concept and adds emphasis.

> **"WHEN WE DO OUR PART TO CULTIVATE AN INTIMATE RELATIONSHIP WITH HIM WE RELEASE THE COVENANT OF PEACE."**

"Consider it **nothing but joy,** *my brothers and sisters, whenever you fall into various trials.* **Be assured** *that the* **testing** *of your faith [through experience]* **produces** *endurance [leading to spiritual maturity, and* **inner peace].** *And let endurance have its perfect result and do a thorough work, so that you may be perfect and completely developed [in your faith], lacking in nothing." (James 1:2-4 AMP)*

James is inviting us to embrace the circumstances that may cause us pain, considering them nothing BUT JOY, because when we are tested, the product is INNER PEACE and rest.

The implication is that when we are challenged and uncomfortable with our circumstances and YET choose to *remain in Christ*, we are creating a habitation for His supernatural peace to overflow. When we instead partner with the distress, we build a house for anxiety, fear, and angst. We may not get to choose our circumstances, but we do get to choose which identity we want to cultivate from those circumstances.

Paul repeats this message in Romans 5:2-5 (AMP):

> *"Through Him we also have* **access by faith** *into this [remarkable state of]* **grace in which we [firmly and safely and securely] stand.** *Let us rejoice in our [a]hope and the confident assurance of [experiencing and enjoying] the glory of [our great] God [the manifestation of His excellence and power]. And not only this, but [with joy] let us exult in our sufferings and rejoice in our hardships, knowing that hardship (distress, pressure, trouble) produces patient endurance; and endurance, proven character (spiritual maturity); and proven character, hope and confident assurance [of eternal salvation].* **Such hope [in God's promises] never disappoints us, because God's love has been abundantly poured out within our hearts through the Holy Spirit who was given to us.**

Jesus is the access to the throne of grace, and He infuses us with confident assurance through the work of the Holy Spirit. We are again reminded that by deciding to abide in Christ and leaning into the Holy Spirit, we can embrace the difficulties because we know that this is preparation for the mission ahead.

GRAM MODELED A JAMES 1 KIND OF FAITH

Notwithstanding all the things that she endured, which would test the faith of the strongest among us, Gram's description of the foundation of her faith is inspiring:

> I try to acknowledge the Lord, even in the little things. I thank God for my health. I thank God for waking me up each morning. There would be nothing, absolutely nothing, that would change my mind or make me not serve the Lord. I spend time meditating on the Lord. I choose to think about the Lord and thank Him for His hand on my life.

Gram chose to cultivate peace and remain undaunted by the surrounding chaos. Gram is proof that rest is not an eternal destination. For some, it is a lifestyle.

If we are going to operate from rest, "be still and know that I am God" cannot be an event or a moment. It has to be a lifestyle. We must learn to abide in Christ, dwell in the secret place, and live under the shadow of the Almighty.

When I married my husband, the pastor suggested using sand instead of the traditional candle. My sand was pink, my husband's was purple, and the pastor had black sand. We each had a vial of our sand and there was one receptacle we used to combine it. I poured some, then my husband, then the pastor, symbolizing God's presence in our mix. Then we all poured together. The process repeated until our vials were empty and the sand was in the main receptacle. In the end, the vase with filled with a beautiful array of colored sand that is now permanently interwoven together. Never again can it be separated into three distinct vials. A beautiful picture that the three-cord strand is not easily broken.

This interconnectedness with Christ is what I believe Paul was referencing when he wrote Colossians chapter two.

> *"Therefore as you have received Christ Jesus the Lord, walk in [union with] Him [reflecting His character in the things you do and say—living lives that lead others away from sin], having been deeply rooted [in Him] and now being continually built up in Him and [becoming increasingly more] established in your faith, just as you were taught, and overflowing in it with gratitude."* (Colossians 2:6-7 AMP)

I love the amplified version of this passage.

1. We received Christ; then
2. We walk in union WITH Him; then
3. We reflect HIS character in the things we say and do; and
4. We are deeply rooted in Him; then
5. We become increasingly more established in our faith; and
6. We overflow with gratitude.

I submit that learning to abide in Him may include reminding ourselves of this truth: We have accepted the Lordship of Jesus and embraced His friendship. Because we are saved, redeemed, and accepted by Him, we desire to become so unified with Him that we are exuding His nature. This is how we confirm and validate that God has invited us to salvation and claimed us as His own (see 2 Peter 1:10.)

Like the sand we used in our wedding ceremony, our lives are so interwoven in Christ's that the natural result is evidence of Him wherever we go. This doesn't mean that we are perfect; it is a process of progressive sanctification which leads into the next step.

Then we become deeply rooted in Him, increasingly more established in our faith. I think the Passion Translation does a great job explaining this a bit more.

> *"In the same way you received Jesus our Lord and Messiah by faith, continue your journey of faith, progressing further into your union with him! Your spiritual roots go deeply into his life as you are continually infused with strength, encouraged in every way. For you are established in the faith you have absorbed and enriched by your devotion to him!"* (Colossians 2:6-7 TPT)

Its description paints beautiful imagery of the process. It says, "continue your journey... progressing further... as you are continually infused with strength, encouraged in every way." All of these descriptors are another way to say abiding in rest is a process, it's a discipline, and it takes practice and training. You are enriched because you are established in the faith. Out of our devotion to Him, we establish habits that reflect Him; this is the covenant relationship. Our intimacy with Him activates the covenant of peace.

The Apostle Peter also describes our union with Christ as a process:

> *"So devote yourselves to lavishly supplementing your faith*

with goodness, and to goodness add understanding, and to understanding add the strength of self-control, and to self-control add patient endurance, and to patient endurance add godliness, and to godliness add mercy toward your brothers and sisters, and to mercy toward others add unending love. Since these virtues are already planted deep within, and you possess them in abundant supply, they will keep you from being inactive or fruitless in your pursuit of knowing Jesus Christ more intimately. But if anyone lacks these things, he is blind, constantly closing his eyes to the mysteries of our faith, and forgetting his innocence—for his past sins have been washed away. For this reason, beloved ones, be eager to confirm and validate that God has invited you to salvation and claimed you as his own. If you do these things, you will never stumble. As a result, the kingdom's gates will open wide to you as God choreographs your triumphant entrance into the eternal kingdom of our Lord and Savior, Jesus the Messiah." (2 Peter 1:5-11 TPT)

Words like "supplement" and "add" illustrate this progressive process in which we become more strengthened and spiritually energized, developing deeper roots in love.[4] As our roots grow down into God's love, we are made strong. As we grow in intimacy with Him, HIS character exudes from us, testifying to/of His goodness to all we encounter.

---

4. Love is another word for "character of Christ," as Galatians 5 says the singular fruit of the Spirit is love embodied by all of the traits that follow in explanation. *"But the fruit produced by the Holy Spirit within you is divine love in all its varied expressions: joy that overflows, peace that subdues..."* (Galatians 5:22-23 TPT)

In the footnotes of 2 Peter 1:7 (TPT), we find these additional insights:

> "It is possible to view this passage like an unfolding of faith. 'Out of your faith will emerge goodness, and out of goodness will emerge understanding (of God), and out of understanding (of God) will emerge inner strength (self-control), and out of inner strength will emerge patient endurance, and out of patient endurance will emerge godliness, and out of godliness will emerge mercy toward your brothers and sisters, and out of mercy will emerge love.' It is also possible to view this passage as a mathematical equation. Faith + goodness = understanding. Goodness + understanding = inner strength. Understanding + inner strength = patience. Inner strength + patience = godliness. Patience + godliness = mercy. And godliness + mercy = love."

In other words, as we abide and remain in Christ, His character in us grows and develops. Also, it is there that we find rest. Consider also Psalm 91:1-2 (AMP):

> "...patience that endures, kindness in action,
> a life full of virtue, faith that prevails,
> gentleness of heart, and strength of spirit.
> Never set the law above these qualities, for they are meant
> to be limitless."

> "He who dwells in the shelter of the Most High will remain secure and rest in the shadow of the Almighty [whose power no enemy can withstand]. I will say of the Lord, 'He is my refuge and my fortress, My God, in whom I trust [with great confidence, and on whom I rely]!'"

Over and over again, we are reminded that rest is experienced when we abide in Christ and model His ways, nature, and character. Psalm 1:1-3 (TPT) is another example:

> *"What delight comes to the one who follows God's ways! He won't walk in step with the wicked, nor share the sinner's way, nor be found sitting in the scorner's seat. His passion is to remain true to the Word of 'I AM,' meditating day and night[5] on the true revelation of light. He will be standing firm like a flourishing tree planted[6] by God's design, deeply rooted by the brooks of bliss, bearing fruit in every season of life. He is never dry, never fainting, ever blessed, ever prosperous."*

Evidence that blessings flow from abiding in Christ isn't merely contained within the Psalms. King Uzziah also experienced the benefit. The Bible says he prospered when he spent time with the Lord.

> *"He continued to seek God in the days of Zechariah, who had understanding through the vision of God; and as long as he sought (inquired of, longing for) the Lord, God caused him to prosper."* (2 Chronicles 26:5 AMP)

And yet we're reminded that the process is not linear. As we

---

5. To meditate on the revelation of light day and night means to meditate 24/7 on what is good and delightful. However, day signifies a period of enlightenment and night signifies a period of obscurity. Both when we have the light of insight and when we seem to be in the dark, meditation is the key to unlock the revelation of God.

6. Or "transplanted." That is, God planted our lives from where we were into a place of blessing. See Psalm 92:13-14 (TPT).

abide in Christ, we become more like Him, and there we find rest. As we endeavor to become more like Christ, our union is more immersive, and there we find rest.

> "The way you counsel me makes me praise you more, for your whispers in the night give me wisdom, showing me what to do next. Because I set you, Yahweh, always close to me, my confidence will never be weakened, for I experience your wraparound presence every moment. My heart and soul explode with joy—full of glory! Even my body will rest confident and secure." (Psalm 16:7-9 TPT)

If you find yourself lacking wisdom, I encourage you to spend time in Proverbs chapter 8. I believe verse 14 (TPT) perfectly sums up the wisdom we find through abiding in Christ: "You will find true success when you find me, for I have insight into wise plans that are designed just for you. I hold in my hands living-understanding, courage, and strength."

I won't recapitulate the entirety of Psalm 119 within these pages, but I encourage you to take a week and meditate on it. This interplay and correlation between abiding in Christ, becoming more like Him, and finding rest is beautifully encapsulated within its verses. The consequences of falling out of rest are also therein described. Let's take a look at a few verses:

> "You're only truly happy when you walk in total integrity, walking in the light of God's Word. What joy overwhelms everyone who keeps the ways of God, those who seek him as their heart's passion!" (Psalm 119:1-2 TPT)

True happiness is only found in walking in the light of God's Word. Joy is found by pursuing intimacy with Him.

"I will give my thanks to you from a heart of love and truth. And every time I learn more of your righteous judgments, I will be faithful to all that your Word reveals—so don't ever give up on me!" (Psalm 119:7-8 TPT)

The psalmist is affirming his commitment to progressing in his relationship with Lord.

"Let me, your servant, walk in abundance of life that I may always live to obey your truth. Open my eyes to see the miracle-wonders hidden in Scripture." (Psalm 119:17-18 TPT)

Here abundant life is equated with a lifestyle of obedience.

"Your commandments are my counselors; your Word is my light and delight!" (Psalm 119:24 TPT)

I feel this truth in my soul. Whenever I am weary, confused, accidentally take the struggle bus, or just need confirmation, His Word counsels, redirects, and re-energizes me.

"Give me revelation about the meaning of your ways so I can enjoy the reward of following them fully. Give me an understanding heart so that I can passionately know and obey your truth. Guide me into the paths that please you, for I take delight in all that you say." (Psalm 119:33—35 TPT)

This is the role of the Holy Spirit we discussed earlier when examining John 14:26 and 16:13.

"You're my place of quiet retreat, and your wraparound presence becomes my shield as I wrap myself in your Word!" (Psalm 119:114 TPT)

Let's hone in on verse 114. This verse sums up the benefit of abiding in Christ. "Quiet retreat," "wraparound presence," "shield," and "wrapped in Your Word" are perfect illustrations of the covenant of peace. The Amplified version says, "You are my hiding place." As I get to know Christ more, as I spend more time in His presence, as I learn to abide, I experience more rest. The quiet retreat. "Be still and know" becomes a lifestyle.

It is this interactive network of processes where we abide and absorb; we pursue and become; we belong and produce; we supplement and add all that we learn to our faith. It is an ongoing process. AND all the while, we are resting, not striving or straining. The beautiful thing is, as we abide in Christ, He also abides in us. John 15:4 (NKJV) says, *"Abide in Me, and I in you."* Paul describes it in 2 Timothy 2:19 (TPT) this way: *"But the firm foundation of God has written upon it these two inscriptions: 'The Lord God recognizes those who are truly his!'"*[7]

WHAT DOES IT LOOK LIKE TO ABIDE?

What does it mean to abide? What does it look like as we go through our daily routines?

It starts with applying the principles that we've discussed so far. It means taking time to acknowledge the Lordship of Jesus in our lives, spending time with Him in prayer, worship, and Bible reading. It is creating a habit of recognizing who you are and who He is, even before a need arises. Something about taking those moments in the morning to align myself, my attitude,

---

7. Numbers 16:5 (AMP): *"and he spoke to Korah and all his company, saying, 'In the morning the Lord will show who belongs to Him, and who is holy, and will bring him near to Himself; the one whom He will choose He will bring near to himself.'"*

my emotions, and my thought processes with Him sets the right atmosphere for me to remain in Him throughout my day.

NOT ABIDING

I had been in a four-month process to obtain a job. I was fully invested. The whole process was a journey. (You will read more about it in Chapters 10 and 11.) In the four-month process, I believe the Lord was teaching me the principles of resting in Him, trusting in Him, leaning not on my own understanding, and truly believing that "Thy will be done." I habitually recommitted the process to the Lord even when I was momentarily distracted and straying from a place of rest.

I ultimately did not get the job. And it was then that I forgot to abide.

All I had were questions. Confusion clouded my perspective. All the things I thought I learned about resting and waiting totally took a vacation. I allowed self-doubt to overwhelm me. For exactly one week, I was a mess. Shame, guilt, and condemnation for being unable to get a grip only worsened matters. I knew the Lord was with me in the process and yet how easily I allowed myself to forget that when things didn't turn out as expected. I didn't lean into Him when the process was over. I didn't give Him my anxious thoughts. I tried to strive, strain, figure out, and explain it to myself.

Exactly one week from the closed door I wasn't expecting, another opened.

I felt like the disciples must have when they were scolded by Jesus on the boat in the storm after all the miracles. (You can find the story in Matthew chapter 8.) Jesus had cleansed the leper, healed the servant (remotely, I might add), healed Peter's mother-in-law, and *"cast out the evil spirits with a word, and restored to health all who were sick"* (Matthew 8:16). Afterward, Jesus was tired from that ministry and fell asleep on the boat. But there was a storm and the disciples were afraid. The same men just witnessed all of those miracles, plus all the ones described in the previous chapters, and yet a little rain had their knees knocking.

> *"And the disciples went and woke Him, saying, 'Lord, save us, we are going to die!' He said to them, 'Why are you afraid, you men of little faith?' Then He got up and rebuked the winds and the sea, and there was [at once] a great and wonderful calm [a perfect peacefulness]. The men wondered in amazement, saying, 'What kind of man is this, that even the winds and the sea obey Him?'"* (Matthew 8:25-27 AMP)

After four months of seeing God's faithfulness in multiple aspects of my life, not to mention the forty years of faithfulness before that, my knees were knocking. It was like I could hear Him saying to me as He did to the disciples, "Why are you afraid? Why are you not resting?"

The other door opened. And it was like He said to me, "Again, Jacklyn, you are not your own source. I AM in control. None of this caught me by surprise. I really do have this. In the process and in the answers, the ones you like and the ones you don't think you like."

I'm sure you also can consider a situation where things didn't quite turn out as you expected or as you had prayed. Instead of resting in the sovereignty of God, you panicked. So we all know what "not abiding" looks like.

ABIDING

While writing this book, I got an unexpected email from the managing partner at my law firm. He wanted to discuss my employment and "renegotiate." It is common in a professional setting for employees or employers to renegotiate employment contracts or compensation structure. It is nevertheless unsettling to receive such a message out of the blue.

I called my husband first. He simply asked me what I was going to do. Before I could think of a response, the words, "I don't have enough information with which to do anything," poured out of my mouth and I had peace. I connected with the prayer partners in my life and simply told them that I got that unexpected email and would they pray that the Lord would go before me. I asked them to pray that with every encounter, I would remember whose I am and who He is; I would not forget that He is my Source.

(Resting and abiding doesn't necessarily mean only me and Jesus against the world. Even Jesus had His friends pray with Him).

Several phone calls with management followed. I maintained my position as a daughter of the King even though the calls were uncomfortable and offered no resolve.

I had to write some emails back to them. Holy Spirit gave me words to say. And just to make sure, He gave me the grace and discipline not to fire those off, but to sleep on it and be deliberate with my words.

As I'm writing this, it has not worked out. But for me, it is. I know that God is in control and I am committed in this process to not allow myself to pick back up a responsibility that is not mine. I am determined that I will not wear the cloak of worry. I am resolved that I am who He says I am, not defined by my job title or salary. He is my Source anyway. It's going to work out.

Abiding means that when the email comes from your boss, when the results come from the doctor, when the call comes from the bank, our response is not fretful or fearful. Our reaction is not a frantic attempt to awake a perceived Jesus sleeping on our boat. Instead, like Jeremiah, we call to mind the enduring faithfulness of Almighty God. We choose to remember all of the times He came through for us before and rest in the knowledge that He is the same God. He is going to come through for us again.

Do you think that when Shadrach, Meshach, and Abednego told the king that God was going to save them, they thought they would be thrown into the fire and survive? I don't. I believe they thought one of two things would happen: either God would spare them altogether or they would go to heaven. Either way, they were going to be faithful to the Faithful God.

When the fire was turned up hotter and they were thrown in and didn't die, I believe they were shocked. That was not the answer they were expecting. And yet, what an awesome answer it was. Jesus was WITH them. They experienced a face-to-face encounter with Jesus in the middle of their trial.

Not one thing catches God by surprise. His plans for you are good. His goodness and mercy follow you all the days of your life. You are blessed and highly favored. You may need an attitude adjustment, but His sovereignty is not affected by your attitude. His faithfulness does not depend on your circumstances.

There are plenty of things that we don't understand (1 Corinthians 13:12). He is not daunted by our questions. Asking God our questions does not mean we are not resting. There's a difference between asking and fretting. There's a difference between confusion and worry. Bring all your petitions to Him (Philippians 4:6). What are petitions? Questions. Requests. Appeals. Complaints. Bring those to Him! Engage in that divine exchange (see chapter 2). Do not allow yourself to focus on the questions. Instead, fasten your thoughts on Jesus. Turn on your worship music. Pray in the shower. Maybe this situation calls for prayer and fasting. You are not held by your own strength. Lean into Him.

Before we dive into the next activation, let's pause for a moment and consider the SOAP Bible study method first developed by Pastor Wayne Cordeiro, which was adopted into the book *Praying with Confidence*, by Pastor Jeff Leake.

S – Scripture
O – Observation
A – Application
P – Prayer

Together, these pastors recommend you choose a Scripture or two and write that at the top of your journal page. Then, Observe or "reflect on what the verse meant at the time it was written to those for whom it was written." Next is Application. After considering what it meant to the original audience, ask Holy Spirit to reveal what He's speaking to you. Finally, Prayer. After contemplating how you can apply the verse(s) to your life or current situation, write a sentence or two as a prayer to the Lord, partnering with these promises in your life.

I invite you to read these verses prayerfully, attuning your ear and your heart to one or two that may specifically speak to you. Then, read the verses a second time. This time, identify the verse(s) that you will focus on. Next, reread that verse(s) and reflect on what it may have meant when it was written. Reread the verse again. This time, consider what Holy Spirit may be revealing to you in this moment. Highlight, underline, or circle a key word or words that seem to jump off the page for you. Record your thoughts and reflections. Finally, reframe what you have gathered into a prayer. It doesn't need to be long; just a sentence or two as a consecration, aligning your heart with the verse(s) and its promises or instructions for your life.

ACTIVATION

If you like the addition of worship with the activation, I invite you to listen to "I Will Fear No More" by The Afters, "Yes I Will" by Vertical Worship. Worship, or "Worthy of My Song" by Phil Wickham, Chandler Moore, and Maverick City Music.

As we apply what we've learned about abiding, I challenge you to pray this prayer with me:

> *Lord, I thank You that You desire to abide in me and that You invite me to abide in You. Help me to be even more vulnerable with You. Uncover to me the areas of my life that I have kept hidden from You. Expose the secret places of my heart so that I may grow in intimacy with You. I desire to make Your words at home in my heart. I yearn to walk so closely in step with You that Your desires are my desires. Holy Spirit, I long to have joy that is mature, full, complete, and overflowing. Reveal to me the steps I must take to experience this infusion of fortitude. Amen.*

1. Are you engaged in a relationship with Christ? Are you growing deeper in your relationship with Him? Does His character and nature ooze out of you when squeezed? Invite the Holy Spirit to identify the ways you need to progress.

_____

_____

_____

_____

_____

_____

2. What are you facing that challenges your courage, confidence, or joy? How are these challenges cultivating endurance and inner peace? What is He revealing about Himself in these challenges? What is He revealing about you?

_____

_____

_____

_____

_____

_____

3. Reread 2 Peter 1:5-11. In what ways is He encouraging you to supplement and add to your faith?

_____

_____

_____

_____

_____

_____

4. Choose one of the following passages: Psalm 119:17-32 or Psalm 119:169-176. Read the entire passage one time through or use the YouVersion Bible app and allow it to read to you. (This may mean that you must listen to the entire chapter.) Write down the word(s), phrase(s), or verse(s) that really stand out to you.

_____

_____

_____

_____

_____

_____

5. Read the entire passage a second time through. This time, ask Holy Spirit what God is revealing to you in this passage. What do you observe?

_____

_____

_____

_____

_____

_____

6. Read the entire passage a third time. Ask Holy Spirit how you can apply what He is speaking to you.

_____

_____

_____

_____

_____

_____

7. Respond to God in prayer and record your prayer in your journal. Partner with the Scripture or the portion(s) that really spoke to you and reword it in the form of a consecration or renewed commitment to apply the truths that you have gleaned.

CHAPTER 8

REST IN ACTION

A LIFESTYLE OF resting in Him is to do as He commands and depend on Him for the rest.

The Lord revealed these truths to Moses in Deuteronomy 28:1-3 (AMP) when he wrote:

> *"Now it shall be, if you diligently listen to and obey the voice of the Lord your God, being careful to do all of His commandments which I am commanding you today, the Lord your God will set you high above all the nations of the earth. All these blessings will come upon you and overtake you if you pay attention to the voice of the Lord your God. You will be blessed in the city, and you will be blessed in the field."*

I encourage you to explore Deuteronomy 28 word by word.

For now, let us meditate on these three verses. In this passage we learn that BLESSINGS WILL OVERTAKE US! Who would reject this measure of blessings? The passage goes deeper, highlighting that we will be blessed when we come and when we go; we are blessed at home or work. The passage reveals the key to unlocking this quality of blessing:

1. Listen: diligently listen to the voice of the Lord
2. Obey: diligently obey the voice of the Lord
3. Do: be careful to do all His commandments

Deuteronomy 28:1-3 promises that if we listen, obey, and do all the Lord commands, He will be faithful to heap upon us blessings that we cannot contain, blessings that overtake us. If you are concerned that this is an Old Testament covenant, these principles were repeated in the New Testament.

The New Testament reiterates the command to listen, obey, and do. Obedience is the act of putting yourself in a position to do what you've been instructed. In other words, obedience is the attitude that precedes the action.

Since listening is the first step. Let's talk about how to position ourselves to hear.

> *"I will climb up to my watchtower and stand at my guardpost. There I will wait to see what the Lord says and how he will answer my complaint."* (Habakkuk 2:1 NLT)

Habakkuk was expecting God to speak to him. So, he decided to put himself in a position to hear from God. Then, he waited for God to speak. Here, we're inviting Holy Spirit to speak to us. This is an exercise to help you practice listening.

I believe that God can and does speak to us in the car, in the shower, at school, at church, at work, etc. It isn't that He doesn't speak unless we are in a certain place; it's that sometimes we cannot hear Him because we're distracted or haven't otherwise put ourselves in the right frame of mind to hear.

Once we hear, it's time to obey and do. If we continue with Habakkuk's model, we should be prepared to write down what we hear.

> *"Then the Lord said to me, 'Write my answer plainly on tablets, so that a runner can carry the correct message to others.'"* (Habakkuk 2:2 NLT)

As we examine the next few verses, I encourage you to engage by underlining, highlighting, or circling the words that resonate with you. Position yourself to allow these instructions to be specific for you. I can sometimes get distracted when I'm reading. But when I discipline myself to engage by taking notes or highlighting, I'm more likely to hear what God may be speaking to me through the verses. Inevitably, if I was careful to engage in active listening, Holy Spirit will remind me later. (All emphasis in the following verses is mine.)

- *"For it's not merely knowing the law that makes you right with God, **but doing** all that the law says that will cause God to pronounce you innocent."* (Romans 2:13 TPT)

- *"'Yes,' said Jesus, 'but God will bless all who **listen** to the word of God and **carefully obey** everything they hear.'"* (Luke 11:28 TPT)

- *"For whoever **does** the will of My Father who is in heaven [by believing in Me, and following Me] is My brother and sister and mother."* (Matthew 12:50 AMP)

- *"We have become his poetry, a recreated people that **will fulfill the destiny he has given each of us**, for we are joined to Jesus, the Anointed One. Even before we were born, God planned in advance our destiny and the good works we would do to fulfill it!"* (Ephesians 2:10 TPT)

- *"For I will not [even] presume to speak of anything except what Christ has done through me [as an instrument in His hands], resulting in the **obedience** of the Gentiles [to the gospel], **by word and deed**, with the power of signs and wonders, [and all of it] in the power of the Spirit. So [starting] from Jerusalem and as far away as Illyricum, I have fully preached the gospel [faithfully preaching the good news] of Christ [where it had not before been preached]."* (Romans 15:18-19 AMP)

- *"I assure you and most solemnly say to you, anyone who believes in Me [as Savior] **will also do** the things that I do; and he will do even greater things than these [in extent and outreach], because I am going to the Father."* (John 14:12 AMP)

Pause here as you engage the S.O.A.P principles discussed above. What is that God has instructed you to do?

When you are ready to dive a bit deeper, let's continue.

I intend not to flood you with verses to fill up the page. We may feel more drawn to or identify with certain words. God is so gracious with us that He gives us His promises in various words with various descriptors. I believe that God repeats His promises and instructions to confirm and confirm again the recipe for abiding in His rest.

God promises blessing upon blessing if we DO what He has instructed us. In so doing, we must be careful to begin from a place of love and rest instead of obligation. We must not forget that we cannot earn the merit and favor of the Lord. Out of our love for Him and our covenant relationship with Him, we recognize the benefits of obedience.

Rest in action from a place of unity with Christ, and out of adoration for Him is not an activity of striving, and straining. When both our hearts and minds are engaged in the covenant of peace, obedience is natural byproduct through the power of the Holy Spirit in us and not of our own strength. (We will explore this further in Chapter 9.)

We must not grow weary in doing good (Galatians 6:9), but remain steady and steadfast in obeying all the Lord has commanded.

I choose to embrace the promise of Isaiah 58:11 (GNT): *"And I will always guide you and satisfy you with good things. I will keep you strong and well. You will be like a garden that has plenty of water, like a spring that never goes dry."* I believe that as I endeavor to honor the Lord and rest in His strength instead of my own, He will constantly guide and redirect me. He will quicken me when I misstep, He will reveal to me the things, thoughts, and people that I need to surrender to Him.

I recognize that the supernatural guidance available to me requires my participation. I must make myself available to receive the instruction and then be willing to walk that out. The Psalmist says it this way:

"Direct me, Yahweh, throughout my journey so I can experience your plans for my life. Reveal the life-paths that are pleasing to you. Escort me into your truth; take me by the hand and teach me. For you are the God of my salvation; I have wrapped my heart into yours all day long." (Psalm 25:4-5 TPT)

"Teach me more about you, how you work and how you move, so that I can walk onward in your truth until everything within me brings honor to your name. With all my heart and passion I will thank you, my God! I will give glory to your name, always and forever!" (Psalm 86:11-12 TPT)

If we do not position ourselves us to receive the instructions, how can we expect to be guided into the plans and purposes God has for us?

Hearing from God and knowing His timing are not the same thing. Sometimes what God reveals to us is a right now instruction. Other times, He is planting seeds in our hearts or giving us vision for the future. Habakkuk advises us about this, too:

"This vision is for a future time. It describes the end, and it will be fulfilled. If it seems slow in coming, wait patiently, for it will surely take place. It will not be delayed." (Habakkuk 2:3 NLT)

For example, what if you felt called to become a doctor? That vision might be for a future time. It requires continually repositioning yourself to be available to do the next step in the process. Maybe it's unclear whether what God spoke to you is for now or later. I invite you to ask the Lord for additional instructions.

Earlier, we discussed being aware of the season that we're in. Graduation from one season to the next always requires faithfulness in the one we're in. I've included some additional verses that reiterate these principles. I implore you to use the S.O.A.P method again, or simply identify, in a way that makes sense to you, the verse(s) or word(s) within the verse(s) that spark something in you. You can come back later and use the S.O.A.P method with these verses.

- *"Therefore, my beloved brothers and sisters, be steadfast, immovable, always excelling in the work of the Lord [always doing your best and doing more than is needed], being continually aware that your labor [even to the point of exhaustion] in the Lord is not futile nor wasted [it is never without purpose]."* (1 Corinthians 15:58 AMP)

- *"Blessed [happy, spiritually prosperous, favored by God] is the man who is steadfast under trial and perseveres when tempted; for when he has passed the test and been approved, he will receive the [victor's] crown of life which the Lord has promised to those who love Him."* (James 1:12 AMP)

- *"So prepare your minds for action, be completely sober [in spirit—steadfast, self-disciplined, spiritually and morally alert], fix your hope completely on the grace [of God] that is coming to you when Jesus Christ is revealed."* (1 Peter 1:13 AMP)

- *"So don't follow me without considering what it will cost you. For who would construct a house before first sitting down to estimate the cost to complete it? Otherwise he may lay the foundation and not be able to finish. The neighbors will ridicule him, saying, 'Look at him! He started to build but couldn't complete it!' Have you ever heard of a commander who goes out to war without first sitting down with strategic planning to determine the strength of his army to win the war against a stronger opponent? If he knows he doesn't stand a chance of winning the war, the wise commander will send out delegates to ask for the terms of peace.*" (Luke 14:28-32 TPT)

- "*Before you do anything, put your trust totally in God and not in yourself. Then every plan you make will succeed.... Within your heart you can make plans for your future, but the Lord chooses the steps you take to get there.*" (Proverbs 16:3, 9 TPT)

- "*All your brilliant wisdom and clever insight will be of no help at all if the Lord is against you. You can do your best to prepare for the battle, but ultimate victory comes from the Lord God.*" (Proverbs 21:30-31 TPT)

You see, we are reminded over and over again that God puts His "super" on our "natural." We do what we can do and God does the rest. In the same way that He met Jonathan when he stepped out in faith in 1 Samuel 14, God also honors our faith. It bears repeating that there are times that we don't know what to do or don't have the strength to do what we think we should. It is in these moments that we must be disciplined to reposition ourselves, recalibrate our mindsets, and once again identify ourselves as co-heirs with Christ. We need to be like David and encourage ourselves in the Lord, refusing to allow ourselves to slip back into a working for the weekend mentality. Remember that His strength is only perfected when we acknowledge our weaknesses, so we lean into Him.

GIULIANA'S EXPERIENCE

My youngest daughter reminded me what embracing the Holy Spirit's work in our lives looks like. She modeled for me what it means to listen, obey, and do as the Lord instructs. We were at church. The sermon had ended and the atmosphere was prayerful as people began to leave. She told me that someone needed prayer for their knee. So I took her hands in mine and prayed for healing in someone's knee.

At that very moment, two ladies were praying at the altar. She interrupted me, "No, Mommy. I mean I need to pray for that lady's knee to be healed." Before I could object, she had gotten up and walked toward the woman. "God told me to pray for your knee. Which one is it?" she confidently asked the lady. When the lady identified the knee, my daughter asked for the oil. Obediently, I handed her the anointing oil I carry in my purse. She anointed the lady with oil and prayed a simple prayer of healing for her knee. Immediately, the lady reported her symptoms were gone. She explained that for years she has had ongoing issues, and for the first time since she can remember, she was pain free.

Before she finished speaking, Giuliana turned to the other lady. "God wants to heal your knee, too!" Sure enough, the other lady had tweaked her knee earlier that day. Giuliana prayed for her, as well. She too reported instantaneously relief.

After she hugged the ladies, we turned to leave. I asked her, "How did you know you needed to pray for those ladies?" Very plainly she retorted, "Because God went boom boom on my knee (as she physically tapped her knee with her hand) and told me they were over there. I knew that meant He was going to heal two knees. Simple."

I felt rebuked. I was nearly dismissive of her indication that someone needed prayer for their knee. In my mind, I was placating her when I just prayed quietly in our seats. But she had heard from God and God used her.

"IT IS IN THESE MOMENTS THAT WE MUST BE DISCIPLINED TO REPOSITION OURSELVES, RECALIBRATE OUR MINDSETS, AND ONCE AGAIN IDENTIFY OURSELVES AS CO-HEIRS WITH CHRIST."

As we were leaving, the first lady chased us down and gave Giuliana such a big hug. She had been praying for years for her knee to be healed. She couldn't believe God used a child. She said softly to Giuliana, "Thank you for being obedient to Jesus."

Listen, obey, and do does not necessarily mean sell all you own and go to the land that God will send you. It may mean listen as God invites you to go pray for a lady's knee. I hope that Giuliana's example will awaken in you the simplicity of obedience to the voice of the Lord. Sometimes, I think we make it a bit more complicated than it actually is, and in a way, we talk ourselves out of obedience.

As we proceed to the next activation, I encourage you to truly invite the Holy Spirit to shine a search light to remind you of the times that He has given you a simple instruction, and that He will awaken you to recognize when those moments come in the future.

ACTIVATION

To enhance your experience, I recommend listening to "Build a Boat" by Colton Dixon or "Confidence" by Sanctus Real.

Position yourself to pray this with me:

> *Holy Spirit, help me to have faith in action. Help me to listen and obey when You speak to me. Quicken me to respond when You instruct me. In Jesus' name, amen.*

Consider the verses we explored above. Use the space below to engage further.

1. Scripture

Write the verse(s) that is speaking loudest to you.

_____

_____

_____

_____

_____

2. Observation

Record your reflections about what the verse(s) meant when it was written.

_____

_____

_____

_____

_____

3. Application

What is Holy Spirit revealing to you about how this verse(s) applies to your life?

_____

_____

_____

_____

_____

4. Prayer

Rewrite your thoughts into a short prayer.

_____

_____

_____

_____

_____

_____

_____

_____

_____

_____

_____

_____

_____

_____

_____

_____

PART THREE

WHY CAN WE REST?

Here, we will explore the power of Holy Spirit to ignite a new paradigm within us. We will discover that God is our Source; it is not up to us. We will examine the biblical promise that we can have the mind of Christ. We will investigate our God-given authority. As we evaluate these tools and decide how to implement them, we will increase our connectivity to Him. In so doing, we will recognize that to be free is to operate from rest.

CHAPTER 9

HOLY SPIRIT

THE BIBLE MAKES clear that the Holy Spirit is the manifestation of peace. From the very beginning, it was Holy Spirit hovering over the chaos.[8] Jesus explained that while He was going to the Father, He was leaving Peace with us.[9] When we look at John 14 and 16 in harmony, we see that the promised peace is Holy Spirit. A modus operandi of rest is only possible through Holy Spirit's presence in our lives.

Paul said this: *"May the God of hope fill you with all joy and peace in believing [through the experience of your faith] that by the power of the Holy Spirit you will abound in hope and overflow with confidence in His promises."* (Romans 15:13 AMP) What does it mean to "abound in hope" and "overflow with confidence"? It is to operate from rest. How can we operate from rest? By and through the power of the Holy Spirit.

---

8. See Genesis 1:1-2.

9. See John 14:25-28 and John 16:7.

Stick with me as we dive a little deeper. First, let's explore Galatians 3:3-5 (TPT):

> "*So answer me this: Did the Holy Spirit come to you as a reward for keeping Jewish laws? No, you received him as a gift because you believed in the Messiah. **Your new life began when the Holy Spirit gave you a new birth.** Why then would you so foolishly turn from living in the Spirit by trying to finish by your own works?*
>
> *Have you endured so many trials and persecutions for nothing? Let me ask you again: What does the **lavish supply** of the Holy Spirit in your life and the miracles of God's tremendous power have to do with you keeping religious laws? The Holy Spirit is poured out upon us through the **revelation and power of faith!**"*

First, can we say 'Amen' and 'Hallelujah'?! Thank You, Jesus, that I undeservedly received the gift of the Holy Spirit! Thank You for the new life I have because of Holy Spirit! God neither expects nor wants us to conduct ourselves from the power of our own strength. Instead, He has given us Himself in the form of the Holy Spirit so that we live through that revelation and faith; from a place of peace and resolve.

"'*Not by might nor power but by My Spirit,' says the Lord.*" (Zechariah 4:6 NIV) My friends, we cannot abide in a posture of rest without the Holy Spirit. There's not enough striving and straining we can do in our abilities to accomplish the plans and purposes that God has for us. He expects us to lean into Him, to be plugged in to the power that only comes from the Holy Spirit.

I submit to you that a life of rest, of abiding peace, begins with Holy Spirit. Paul describes the quantity of the equipping from Him as one in "lavish supply." *Lavish* means profusely, in abundance, in excess, overflowing, "in great amounts without limit."[8]

Sometimes we talk about quantity or levels in terms of faith; for example, "faith the size of a mustard seed." What if we took that valuation a step further as we consider the measure of the power of the Holy Spirit that we tap into and allow to flow through our lives? Are we allowing a "lavish supply" of the Holy Spirit's character, nature, and power to work in and through our lives? This means there are no circumstances, situations, people, emotions, thoughts, or processes which have the authority to exceed the overarching presence of Holy Spirit. Are we tapping in to that measure of Holy Spirit power?

Now let's look again at Ephesians 3:16-19 (AMP):

> *"May He grant you out of the riches of His glory, to be strengthened and spiritually energized with **power through His Spirit** in **your inner self**, [indwelling your innermost being and personality], so that Christ may dwell in your hearts through your faith. And may you, having been [deeply] rooted and [securely] grounded in love, be fully capable of comprehending with all the saints (God's people) the width and length and height and depth of His love [fully experiencing that amazing, endless love]; and [that you may come] to know [practically, through personal experience] the love of Christ which far surpasses [mere] knowledge [without experience], that you may be filled up [throughout your being] to all the fullness of God [so that you may have the richest experience of God's presence in your lives, **completely filled and flooded with God Himself**]."*

For our discussion about the Holy Spirit's role in abiding peace, let's examine verse 16. Holy Spirit's equipping power dwells within our innermost being and personality. Once again, we are reminded that it is not through our skills, trying, or work that we are strengthened or spiritually energized. In our natural personalities, we cannot abide in the rest that only comes through the power of His Spirit. And this equipment is nothing insignificant. Verse 19 says, "completely filled and flooded."

> **"THE HOLY SPIRIT IS SUCH A CRITICAL INGREDIENT IN THE RECIPE FOR PEACE THAT JESUS INSTRUCTED THE DISCIPLES TO WAIT FOR IT BEFORE THEY SET OUT TO DO AS HE HAD CALLED THEM."**

Paul describes the "richest experience of God's presence."

The third Person of the Trinity, Holy Spirit, manifests God's presence. How can we operate from a place of peace? By operating in the fullness of Christ. How can we experience the fullness of Christ? Through the power of the Holy Spirit.

The Holy Spirit is such a critical ingredient in the recipe for peace that Jesus instructed the disciples to wait for it BEFORE they set out to do as He had called them:

> *"What comes next is very important: I am sending what my Father promised to you, so stay here in the city until **he** arrives, until you're equipped with power from on high."* (Luke 24:49 MSG)

In Acts 1:4, the command is a bit stronger: *"Do not leave... but wait for the Promise."* You see, the disciples had an impossible assignment: *"Be my witnesses in Jerusalem, all over Judea and Samaria, even to the ends of the world"* (Acts 1:8 MSG). They were tasked with carrying the good news to their city, state, country, and the world. But Jesus knew that assignment could not be accomplished without the right equipment. It was as if He was saying, "What you'll get is the Holy Spirit. And when the Holy Spirit comes on you, you will be able to be My witnesses in Jerusalem, all over Judea and Samaria, even to the ends of the world." In other words, "You won't be able to do what I have called you to do without the Holy Spirit."

First Peter 1:3 (NIV) says, *"His divine power has given us everything we need for a godly life through our knowledge of Him who called us by His own glory and goodness."* We have all that we need to accomplish our assignments only through the power of the Spirit. The word *power* refers to Greek word *dunamis.* It means "ability to perform, capacity to achieve or accomplish."[9] Without the power of the Holy Spirit, we do not have the ability to do what God has called us to do.

We discussed peace being a product of a lifestyle of prayer and meditation on heavenly things. Peace is also a product of the infilling and overflowing power of the Holy Spirit.[10] The renewal that comes through Holy Spirit's power is not a one-time event. The Day of Pentecost served only as the initial enduement of the Spirit's power. What followed for the disciples was a lifestyle of receiving continual infusions of supernatural energy. (Refer back to chapter 7.) It is not a one and done thing. Ephesians 5:18 instructs us to be filled continually, to keep on being filled with the power of the Holy Spirit.

---

10. For additional resources about the baptism in the Holy Spirit: *What The Bible Says About the Holy Spirit*, Stanley Horton, Gospel Publishing House, 2005. | *The Holy Spirit: An Introduction* by John Bevere, Messenger International, 2014. | *How to be Filled with the Holy Spirit*, AW Tozer Series Book 6, Gromedia, 2021. | *Filled with the Spirit*, Joyce Meyer, Hachette Nashville, 2008.

ACTIVATION

I suggest playing "Spirit of the Living God" by Vertical Worship or "Fullness" by Elevation Worship for a more immersive activation.

To apply what we've learned in this chapter, let's start with an intentional prayer. Maybe that prayer sounds something like this:

> *Holy Spirit, I invite You to reveal Yourself to me right now in a deeper way. I want to experience the fullness of God's presence in my life. I lean into You for spiritual strength and energy. I desire a fresh encounter with the peace Jesus promised to the disciples. Help me relinquish any faulty beliefs or misconceptions about who You are. Release a fresh outpouring right now, in Jesus' name, amen.*

1. As you linger in this posture of prayer, begin to thank the Lord for who He is in your life. Thank Him for the ways that He has already revealed Himself to you.

_____

_____

_____

_____

_____

2. Invite Him to stir up the gifts within you. Allow Him to fill you afresh and anew. Take a moment to express your love and adoration for Him.

_____

_____

_____

_____

_____

_____

3. Invite Holy Spirit to partner with you in divine exchange as you exchange any constraints or restrictions on what you will allow Him to do in your life with complete surrender.

_____

_____

_____

_____

_____

4. If sounds come to your spirit and out of your mouth in a language you don't understand, that's okay; that's the power of the Holy Spirit. Engage with that a little more. That is the Holy Spirit operating inside of you. Linger here for a few more moments.

_____

_____

_____

_____

_____

5. Write down some thoughts about this experience. Record what God has revealed to you in these moments.

_____

_____

_____

_____

_____

_____

Before we go, let's pray to seal the work that Holy Spirit is doing.

Holy Spirit, thank You for revealing Yourself to me, for filling me to overflowing with Your power and presence. I invite You to continue Your work in me perpetually. I desire to be completely filled and flooded by Your Spirit. Thank You for protecting the fertile soil of my heart and the deposits that are made as I commune with You. Help me abide in the rest Jesus promised. Amen.

CHAPTER 10

GOD IS MY SOURCE

IN JUNE 2022, I went to Italy with my daughter. It was the first time I had been there since my father died. When I arrived at my parents' home, grief overwhelmed me. He wasn't there. And yet I had this peace. I felt purposeful.

Since I was preaching Sunday, mom thought it would be best to visit the church beforehand.

Seeing the flags and the photos, my father's fingerprints were everywhere.

When we arrived on Sunday, we were greeted by so many; so many who loved my father. He'd be so proud of all of them. As I preached for the services on Sunday, it was as if he was with me. And, for the first time in a long time, I felt called. Afterward, a couple Italian parishioners greeted me and explained how I reminded them of my father. I encouraged them with my father's favorite phrase: God's Got This. And ultimately, I gave them the bracelet I wore, which bore the same inscription.

It was as if I felt a seed sprout inside of me. God was doing something new.

Then, it was kids camp. I was so proud of the whole team. Every worker, leader, and volunteer reflected the training and mentorship of my parents. The joyful singing and dancing of the children, I could almost see my father joining in.

For the first time since we had moved to Kansas, I felt "unsettled," almost like I would soon be getting some instructions.

My daughter, while at home, is one of three. Here, she was in a whole new element. What had been quite a challenging school year was left in the dust by the courage and independence she exhibited in Italy. Engaging with children, raising their hands, dancing with them, sharing the love of Jesus... she experienced what it means to let her light shine. It wasn't long before she started saying how much she loved it there and didn't want to leave. What was God up to?

It was time for me to go home. On the trip home, I held an open attitude or posture of listening to Lord. What was He trying to tell me in Italy? What was that "new thing" it seemed like He was doing?

I asked Him if I needed to get home and work on a visa or citizenship documentation.

I felt no urgency in that direction. I did, however, feel like we needed to go back to Italy—soon. This time with the whole family.

(Our flight had been canceled on the way there. Delta asked volunteers to stay in Boston two extra days and gave us money to do so. Ultimately, they refunded the cost of the original tickets. This money could then be used to purchase tickets for the whole family to return to Italy.)

With pressure from my daughter, who used every FaceTime call with my husband to persuade him that we had to go back, and Delta covering the expense, my husband agreed we'd return in December. I didn't hesitate to purchase the tickets. Is this what God was doing?

I had come home from Italy in time to send my 13-year-old on his first missions trip, without us, to Alaska. My dad was for sure so proud of him. The airport send off felt like a culmination. I didn't have words to describe how I felt. Maybe as a family we would be headed toward mission work.

While he was in Alaska, I received an email that my jurisdiction sought two candidates for two new judge positions. I had seen such emails in the past, but they pertained to positions requiring us to be willing to move. I would jokingly ask my husband if we wanted to move so I could be a judge. But this time was different. It was sort of like a neon sign: apply here.

(I had been a licensed attorney for ten years and met all the qualifications. I wanted to be a judge in Michigan, but the process was by election. I never wanted to campaign for political office, so it was nothing I ever pursued. Here, it was by nomination and appointment; it felt like something I needed to do.)

Giovanna was in Italy; Rocco was in Alaska. My husband and I got to spend some one-on-one time with Giuliana.

Then, we were headed to Florida to retrieve Giovanna. She flew back from Italy with my mom. We all went to Florida to support Rocco during national fine arts festival. He had advanced from the state competition where he competed in short sermon and photography. It wasn't an opportune time to gather the information to submit my nomination. So, I decided we would wait until we returned from Florida.

What started as a gentle internal unsettling in Italy was wholly magnetic in Orlando. I felt a stirring, a calling unlike any I had experienced since childhood. But it was like when God called Abraham to leave Ur of the Chaldees. I just couldn't shake the question, "Will you say yes to what I call you to?" When I would attempt to say, "Yes, what can I do?" I would only feel the same question again. Ultimately, it was just sort of this knowing. I messaged a couple dear friends: "Will you pray with me? I feel a stirring like I haven't felt since childhood. I don't know what it means. But I commit to say yes. Obviously, I'm gonna need some instructions, but at the moment all I'm feeling asked for is a 'yes.' He has my 'yes.'"

When we returned from Florida, I had this compulsion to complete the packet for the nominating committee for the judgeships. I had to overnight the packet so it could reach the Supreme Court by the Friday deadline. On Monday, August 15, I received the approval. I would be advanced to a public interview from which the nominating commission would send names to the governor for appointment. All of a sudden, mentors in my life started saying things about "justice," "judicial," "high places," that God was calling me to greater. I felt like God gave me a couple verses:

> *"The Lord God is my strength [my source of courage, my invincible army]; He has made my feet [steady and sure] like hinds' feet And makes me walk [forward with spiritual confidence] on my high places [of challenge and*

responsibility]. For the choir director, on my stringed instruments." (Habakkuk 3:19 AMP)

"Then you will take pleasure in the Lord, And I will make you ride on the high places of the earth, And I will feed you with the [promised] heritage of Jacob your father; For the mouth of the Lord has spoken." (Isaiah 58:14 AMP)

On October 5, my husband came with me to the courthouse where the public interview was held. He was with me when the Supreme Court Justice called to express how impressed she was, and the entire nominating committee was, with my interview. They had decided to recommend me and three others to the governor to fill the positions. I couldn't believe it. I was so proud of myself. I was simply excited I had made it this far, and whether she appointed me or not, I would have a meeting with the governor. I had never met a governor.

I soaked up the celebration for a couple days, then decided to check the details. How much is the salary, benefits, staff, job responsibilities? I quickly learned that the salary would mean a significant pay cut. Suddenly, I panicked.

But then... I heard that voice again: *"Will you say yes to whatever I ask you to do?"*

"THIS? This is what You're asking me?"

"Yes. But it's not up to me. I cannot appoint myself."

"Then the Lord raised up judges." (Judges 2:16 NIV)

"Okay, Lord. I'm available."

The next day, a colleague called after learning I was being considered. I expressed my concern about the money. To my knowledge, he and I don't share the same faith that God is our

Source. And yet, he said, "Jacklyn, the money will come. I have always thought you'd make an incredible judge. I just knew that one day, you would be a judge."

God knew I needed that kind of confirmation.

Then I received the call from the governor's office, congratulating me on my nomination. They would send another set of documents for me to fill out and there would be more information I would need to gather.

I received the documents. And I panicked.

Jobs and coworkers, homes and neighbors... the information requested wasn't information readily available to me. I contemplated withdrawing. My feelings were similar to, "Lord, I believe, help my unbelief."

I gathered myself and completed the documents as best as I could.

I decided to sleep on it one more night and pray one more time to confirm I was obeying by continuing the process.

I overnighted the documents the next day.

The weight of doing so hit me like a ton of bricks. My brain was like marshmallows.

While I intended to work a full day in the office, I called my husband and told him how weary I felt. He was so understanding; supernatural peace and comfort exuded from him.

Then I felt like the Lord gave me another verse:

"The confidence of my calling enables me to overcome every difficulty without shame, for I have an intimate revelation of this God. And my faith in him convinces me that he is more than able to keep all that I've placed in his hands safe and secure until the fullness of his appearing."
(2 Timothy 1:12 TPT)

On November 4, I made it to the first interview with the governor's office. I had supernatural confidence and poise. Never have I ever felt so resolved during an interview.

Jesus helps.

And yet, the next step would be an interview with the Kansas Bureau of Investigations. I was apprehensive only because I worried I hadn't remembered every job or every address. But all in all, I knew I had no reason not to pass or clear a background check. I encouraged myself.

But then... Saturday. I was home with my two daughters snuggling in my bed because it was cold. The girls were fussing with each other a bit. I sent Giuliana outside to let the chickens and other animals out. It was her chore for the weekend. She had done it dozens of times.

When ten minutes passed and she didn't return, I went outside to find all the animals still locked up. Where could she have gone? I looked for her in the barn, the garage, by the duck cage, and in the horse stalls. I assumed I must have missed her going back in. So I went back in the house. Upstairs and down, shouting her name, nothing.

Back outside, I checked the cars, every stall, the RV, the tack room, the front yard, shouting her name. Now I was certain she was hiding in the house. I went back in, this time checking every closet, bathroom, bed, and bedroom frantically shouting her name.

I called my husband to let him know I couldn't find her. Maybe he knew her favorite hiding spot. He told me he had cut new trails through the woods and maybe she was out back exploring, or maybe she chased a cat or something.

I couldn't find her.

I hurried through every trail, every barn and outbuilding. I called my husband back, advising I would now check all the ponds. Maybe she chased a cat and got stuck or fell in or something, but if I didn't find her, I would have to call the police. On my way to check the third pond, my husband was still on the phone when two law enforcement SUVs came speeding down the road. I hadn't called them yet, and they were coming. My heart sank.

What has to happen that warrants a visit and not a phone call?

They seemed to move in slow motion.

Finally, they were at the driveway and I saw her safe in the front passenger seat of the cruiser. I collapsed. Where was she?! The second cruiser stopped. The officer explained that Giuliana told them she was walking ten miles from the house to church. And because they had her, I would have to go to the station to answer some questions before releasing her to me. I went to the station and got her back.

Before any other job, I am first a mom. So many emotions. I didn't think she was lost.

She was lost.

Walk to the church?!

She was found!

I asked, "Giuliana, why did you think you were going to walk to the church?"

She retorted, "Well, I knew how to get there and I needed to pray."

Someone has to help me with this child.

She continued, "Jesus went to the church to pray." Sigh.

I replied, "Sweetheart, you do not have to go somewhere to pray. You can just pray. You can go in your room. You can go in your closet if you need to. You can just start talking wherever you are. Jesus prayed in a lot of places."

Hugs. So many hugs.

Combined in the host of emotions was also a realization that KBI was currently investigating me. Of course, I was glad she was safe. But I also convinced myself the judgeship had sailed. Exasperated, I simply prayed, "Thy will be done." Panic gave way to reason and I again reassured myself that God sets the judges. Surely a headstrong seven-year-old from the country thinking she's walking to church to pray isn't going affect the judge appointment.

On Wednesday, the school called. Rocco was in an "altercation" at school. Bullies put their hands on Rocco and stole his lunch and he hit back. The school wanted me to know the mother was considering pressing charges.

Wait, what? They bullied him. It was two against one. They stole his lunch and put their hands on him and simply because he was bigger and stronger, he was the bad guy. Sigh. They should have realized his size when they picked on him. His muscles were readily apparent to all. How about they don't steal his lunch and put their hands on him? Maybe next time, they will pick on someone their own size, or better yet, think twice before they pick on someone at all.

Annoyance at the injustice and the process gave way to yet another notion that the judgeship had sailed.

I recommitted my children and my future to Lord and again prayed, "Thy will be done."

KBI came to the house and asked me all sorts of questions, leaving me to again convince myself the judgeship sailed. And once again, all I could do was pray, "Thy will be done."

Even though I believe I've learned what it is to abide in rest, I've also learned that it is a choice—sometimes daily, sometimes multiple times a day. It's natural to fret, worry, and overthink things; natural to forget Who really is our Source. It's easy, or I dare say habit, to act, think, believe that it is in our strength, power, and wisdom that we provide for ourselves. It takes discipline to acknowledge when we step outside of rest, when we step into self. Then it takes courage and fortitude to forsake (turn off or mute) a natural/human thought process and return to supernatural rest. God has a way of reminding us that it is not by power, nor by might but only by His Spirit.

In these moments, I became fully prepared to be at peace with whomever the governor appointed to become the judges.

Initially, I was proud of myself, that I had made it past the nomination process and that the committee chose me and three others out of the pool of candidates to submit to the governor. I got that peace back. That was a huge accomplishment. I would get to meet with the governor; not many people get that opportunity. Plus, this was a lesson in being wholly reliant.

I had taught myself to be private, to protect myself, but in this process, all was laid bare. Had it been even two years prior, when I realized how exposed and vulnerable the process would be, I would have pulled my name from consideration and abandoned it. Here, I really learned what it was to rest and trust that God ordains my path and He will provide the fortitude needed for His processes.

"And as your days are, so will your strength, your rest and secu-

rity be" (Deuteronomy 33:25 AMP). God knows what we will face before we face it. He provides before we get there. He equipped us for the day before it arrived. He goes before us.

I was ready for my interview with the governor and excited that my husband could accompany me. Whatever the outcome, God WAS in control. It was pretty cool to meet the governor. She explained that she had lived in Michigan for a bit not too far from where I grew up. We had a great conversation, then the time set aside for our meeting elapsed. I simply felt resolved when we left: "Thy will be done."

I got the call the next day. She had chosen two of the other candidates. It had been a roller coaster, but I was at peace with it all. I fully believe God's plans are better than ours and His ways are higher. Lessons in the process are way more valuable than obtaining the desired outcome.

When we fully understand that God is our Source, verses that explain this are given new meaning.

For example, Jesus said in John 16:33 (AMP), *"I have told you these things, so that in Me you may have [perfect] peace. In the world you have tribulation and distress and suffering, but be courageous [be confident, be undaunted, be filled with joy]; I have overcome the world." [My conquest is accomplished, My victory abiding.]"*

Perfect peace. *Perfect* is defined as "having all the required or desirable elements, qualities, or characteristics;" "as good as it is possible to be;" "absolute; complete." Jesus promised that IN Him, we would have "perfect peace." Unfortunately, we don't always avail ourselves to that promise and often step outside that covenant. Instead, we rely on ourselves more than we ought. He encouraged us to be "undaunted and filled with joy" in everything. When we are IN Him, we recognize He is in complete control even when we don't understand, even when things don't turn out or look exactly as we expected.

The promise that God is our Source is enduring. This Covenant is repeated throughout scripture:

- *"The Lord will guide you continually, giving you water when you are dry and restoring your strength. You will be like a well-watered garden, like an ever-flowing spring."* (Amen!) (Isaiah 58:11 NLT)

- *"The Lord is good, a strength and stronghold in the day of trouble; He knows [He recognizes, cares for, and understands fully] those who take refuge and trust in Him."* (Nahum 1:7 AMP)

- *"The Lord God is my strength [my source of courage, my invincible army]; He has made my feet [steady and sure] like hinds' feet And makes me walk [forward with spiritual confidence] on my high places [of challenge and responsibility]. For the choir director, on my stringed instruments."* (Habakkuk 3:19 AMP)

- *"The Lord is my strength and my [impenetrable] shield; My heart trusts [with unwavering confidence] in Him, and I am helped; Therefore my heart greatly rejoices, And with my song I shall thank Him and praise Him. The Lord is their [unyielding] strength, And He is the fortress of salvation to His anointed."* (Psalm 28:7-8 AMP)

- *"Never doubt God's mighty power to work in you and accomplish all this. He will achieve infinitely more than your greatest request, your most unbelievable dream, and exceed your wildest imagination! He will outdo them all, for his mi-*

raculous power constantly energizes you." (Ephesians 3:20 TPT)

- *"And my God will liberally supply (fill until full) your every need according to His riches in glory in Christ Jesus."* (Philippians 4:19 AMP)

The repeating message is that when our hope and confidence is in Jesus, we are helped, comforted, and strengthened. The truth is, repetition is sometimes education. It's not really a "fake it til you make it" type thing. It's more of an acknowledgment that the tongue has the power of life and death. The Word of God is life giving (John 6:63). You see, these verses contain the promises I repeated to myself and committed to memory. It's amazing how much life and hope they gave me. The bottom line is, no matter the outcome, God is in complete control. Nothing, not one thing, not one outcome catches Him by surprise. When we completely trust in Him and walk in obedience as He directs, we understand what it means to have that perfect peace Jesus promised.

> **"THE REPEATING MESSAGE IS THAT WHEN OUR HOPE AND CONFIDENCE IS IN JESUS, WE ARE HELPED, COMFORTED, AND STRENGTHENED."**

Let us take a look at our part in allowing God to be our source:

- *"Seek the Lord [search diligently for Him and regard Him as the foremost necessity of your life], All you humble of the land Who have practiced His ordinances and have kept His commandments; Seek righteousness, seek humility [regard them as vital]. Perhaps you will be hidden [and pardoned and rescued] In the day of the Lord's anger."* (Zephaniah 2:3 AMP)

- *"For thus says the Lord to the house of Israel, "Seek Me [search diligently for Me and regard Me as more essential than food] so that you may live."* (Amos 5:4 AMP)

- *"And he commanded Judah to seek the Lord God of their fathers [to inquire of and for Him and seek Him as a vital necessity], and to observe the law [given to Moses] and the commandment."* (2 Chronicles 14:4 AMP)

- *"He answered, 'The Scriptures say: Bread alone will not satisfy, but true life is found in every word that constantly goes forth from God's mouth.'"* (Matthew 4:4 TPT)

We trigger the provision of God when we make it our habit to connect and commune with Him. When we obey the instructions of Matthew and seek Him first, all will be provided: *"But first and most importantly seek (aim at, strive after) His kingdom and His righteousness [His way of doing and being right- the attitude and character of God], and all these things will be given to you also."* (Matthew 6:33 AMP)

ACTIVATION

To enhance your experience, I recommend listening to "Protector" by Kim Walker-Smith or "Jireh" by Maverick City.

I invite you to partner your faith with mine and allow the work of the Holy Spirit in your heart and mind to increase your faith as you pray this prayer:

> Lord, I thank You that You are my Source, even when I don't see it, even when I struggle to believe it. When I doubt, when I fail to focus on You instead of my situation, I thank You that You are gracious to remind me. I thank You that Your strength is perfected in my weakness. Help me to recognize Your care and concern for me, even in what I perceive to be unanswered prayers. Help me to have unwavering confidence in You. Enable me to truly find refuge and sustenance in You. Thank You for steadying my feet. Thank You that Your Holy Spirit supplies the courage for me to follow where You lead me and to listen to Your instructions even when it feels uncomfortable. Heighten my senses so that I can be more aware of Your provision in every area of my life. In Jesus' name, amen.

1. Consider the following passage. Read the entire passage one time through or use the YouVersion Bible app and allow it to read to you. (This may mean that you must listen to the entire chapter.) Write down the word(s), phrase(s), or verse(s) that really stand out to you.

""This is why I tell you to never be worried about your life, for all that you need will be provided, such as food, water, clothing—everything your body needs. Isn't there more to your life than a meal? Isn't your body more than clothing?

"Consider the birds—do you think they worry about their existence? They don't plant or reap or store up food, yet your heavenly Father provides them each with food. Aren't you much more valuable to your Father than they? So, which one of you by worrying could add anything to your life?

"And why would you worry about your clothing? Look at all the beautiful flowers of the field. They don't work or toil, and yet not even Solomon in all his splendor was robed in beauty like one of these! So if God has clothed the meadow with hay, which is here for such a short time and then dried up and burned, won't he provide for you the clothes you need—you of little faith?

"So then, forsake your worries! Why would you say, 'What will we eat?' or 'What will we drink?' or 'What will we wear?' For that is what the unbelievers chase after. Doesn't your heavenly Father already know the things your bodies require?

"So above all, constantly seek God's kingdom and his righteousness, then all these less important things will be given to you abundantly. Refuse to worry about tomorrow, but deal with each challenge that comes your way, one day at a time. Tomorrow will take care of itself."" (Matthew 6:25-34 TPT)

_____

_____

_____

_____

_____

_____

2. Read the entire passage a second time through. This time, ask Holy Spirit what God is revealing to you in this passage. What do you observe?

_____

_____

_____

_____

_____

_____

3. Read the entire passage a third time. Ask Holy Spirit how you can apply what He is speaking to you.

_____

_____

_____

_____

_____

_____

4. Respond to God in prayer and record your prayer in your journal. Partner with the Scripture or the portion(s) that really spoke to you and reword it in the form of a consecration or renewed commitment to apply and walk out the truths that you have gleaned.

_____

_____

_____

_____

_____

_____

5. Use a note card or sticky note and write the verse in a place that you will see it often and consider committing it to memory.

CHAPTER 11

THE MIND OF CHRIST

W HEN LIVING OUR lives from a position of rest, we think differently. Having the mind of Christ doesn't have to be a momentary phenomenon. As we abide in Him, we can operate with the mind of Christ.

Second Corinthians 10:5 says, *"We are destroying sophisticated arguments and every exalted and proud thing that sets itself up against the [true] knowledge of God, and we are taking every thought and purpose captive to the obedience of Christ."* Other translations use language like deceptive fantasies, imaginations, pretensions, and arrogance that ought to be exchanged for the true knowledge of God. Paul's verbiage connotes action on our part. We *are* destroying. We *are* presently engaged in demolishing faulty thinking. As we pray without ceasing and make our lives a prayer, every time the enemy infects our thoughts, we fight those until they are no more. We may not be able to control all of our circumstances, but we have the authority to determine what and how we will think. The PHILLIPS paraphrased Bible puts it this way: *"We even fight to capture every thought __until__ it acknowledges the authority of Christ."* Think about that for a moment. We fight to capture. We must discipline ourselves to take captive the thoughts and emotions contrary to Christ's true nature each time they arise. We fight them until they are silenced.

In his letter to the church in Rome, Paul expounds on this instruction: *"And do not be conformed to this world [any longer with its superficial values and customs], but be transformed and progressively changed [as you mature spiritually] by the renewing of your mind [focusing on godly values and ethical attitudes], so that you may prove [for yourselves] what the will of God is, that which is good and acceptable and perfect [in His plan and purpose for you]"* (Romans 12:2 AMP). Again, his language paints the picture of a process, an ongoing commitment to *be* transformed and *progressively* changed, even linking it with the process of sanctification (as you mature spiritually). He goes on to say "by the renewing," another reference to an evolutionary course, as opposed to a one-time event.

The New Living Translation is a little more direct: *"Don't copy the behavior and customs of this world, but let God* transform *you into a new person __by__ changing the way you think. Then you will learn to know God's will for you, which is good and pleasing and perfect"* (Romans 12:2 NLT). This is pretty powerful stuff. If you change your mind, you change your self. If you allow God to transform your mind, in so doing, you will become a new person. Only when you change how you think can you change how you operate.

Let me see if we can break it down even further. The PHIL-LIPS paraphrased Bible says it this way: *"Let God re-mold your minds from within, so that you may prove in practice that the plan of God for you is good."* Re-mold paints a picture of the potter's wheel. Imagine your mind on that wheel, being reshaped and refashioned, impurities and rough places removed, smoothed out into the image intended by the Creator.

In this process, you will experience that God is good to a degree you had not yet experienced, that truly His goodness, mercy, and unfailing love pursue you every moment of your life. When you partner with Holy Spirit to revolutionize the way that you think, you will begin to abide in a place of rest.

When Jeremiah was bemoaning in utter anguish, he had the discipline to *"call to mind"* the faithfulness of an almighty God[11] (Lamentations 3:21). He chose to take captive every thought that did not line up with the character of Christ. The enemy knows that if he can get us to think a certain way, he could get us to feel a certain way, which may lead us to act a certain way. Thoughts are weapons. Paul knew this all too well and took care to admonish us. He told the church at Philippi:

> *"Finally, believers, whatever is true, whatever is honorable and worthy of respect, whatever is right and confirmed by God's word, whatever is pure and wholesome, whatever is lovely and brings peace, whatever is admirable and of good repute; if there is any excellence, if there is anything*

---

11. Lamentations 3:21-23 (NIV) "Yet this I call to mind and therefore I have hope: Because of the Lord's great love we are not consumed, for his compassions never fail. They are new every morning; great is your faithfulness."

worthy of praise, think continually on these things [center your mind on them, and implant them in your heart]." (Philippians 4:8 AMP)

Like Jeremiah, Paul knew it takes discipline to choose what you think about even in situations you cannot change. When we diligently recognize the thoughts, mindsets, and feelings that do not conform to the instructions of Philippians 4:8, we can engage the process outlined in Romans 12:2.

You cannot change what you won't acknowledge. As you learn to abide in Christ, the quickening of Holy Spirit will become more immediate, especially as we learn to respond quickly to those nudges.

I've heard preachers say "delayed obedience is disobedience." The truth is, delaying our response or delaying corrective action at the conviction of the Holy Spirit seems to also turn the volume down on His voice. Each time we ignore or dismiss His promptings, we make it more difficult to hear Him the next time.

On the other hand, as we learn to listen and respond quickly, the volume of His voice seems to get louder, making it easier for us to hear and respond. For me, anyway, it seems that when I listen and obey, He is quick to give me the next instruction. When I make excuses, ignore, or disregard it, the distance or time between instructions seems to grow.

Sometimes I wonder what God would have me do, only to be reminded that I failed to heed the last instruction. I have had to go back to the last instruction I remember and engage there as best as possible to position myself to receive additional guidance.

WE HAVE THE MIND OF CHRIST

Let's look at 1 Corinthians 2:12-16 together:

*Now we have not received the spirit [that belongs to] the world, but the [Holy] Spirit Who is from God, [given to us] that we might **realize** and **comprehend** and **appreciate** the gifts [of divine favor and blessing so freely and lavishly] bestowed on us by God.*

*And we are setting these truths forth in words not taught by human wisdom but **taught by the [Holy] Spirit**, combining and interpreting spiritual truths with spiritual language [to those who possess the Holy Spirit]. But the natural, nonspiritual man does not accept or welcome or admit into his heart the gifts and **teachings** and **revelations of the Spirit of God**, for they are folly (meaningless nonsense) to him; and he is incapable of knowing them [of progressively recognizing, understanding, and becoming better acquainted with them] because they are **spiritually discerned** and **estimated** and **appreciated**.*

But the spiritual man tries all things [he examines, investigates, inquires into, questions, and discerns all things], yet is himself to be put on trial and judged by no one [he can read the meaning of everything, but no one can properly discern or appraise or get an insight into him].

*For who has known or understood the mind (the counsels and purposes) of the Lord so as to guide and instruct Him and give Him knowledge? But **we have the mind of Christ (the Messiah) and do hold the thoughts (feelings and purposes) of His heart.*** (1 Corinthians 2:12-16 AMPC)

In verse 12, circle *realize, comprehend,* and *appreciate.* Holy Spirit enables us to grasp that we are blessed and highly favored. This first verse included three different expressions of mental transactions. Verse 13 goes on to say these spiritual truths are *taught* by Holy Spirit. If Holy Spirit is teaching, then we are learning, engaging in another activity of the mind.

Verse 14 describes the phenomenon as **discern[ing], estimat[ing],** and **appreciat[ing]** the **teachings *and* revelations of the Spirit of God**. This is the second time in the passage that we discover the word "appreciate." Let's take a closer look at that word. Webster's dictionary defines it as follows: to grasp the nature, worth, quality, or significance of; to value or admire highly; to judge with heightened perception or understanding; and to recognize with gratitude. So, Holy Spirit enables us to both grasp and be thankful for the transformation of our minds.

> "OPERATING FROM A PLACE OF REST WITH THE MIND OF CHRIST MEANS BEING INTENTIONAL ABOUT HOW WE ALLOW OUR MIND TO WORK."

Through Holy Spirit, we **examine, investigate, inquire into, question, and discern kingdom revelations.** What does all of that mean? It means **we *have* the *mind of Christ; we possess* the *thoughts* (feelings and purposes) of *His heart*. Wow!** What if we could take hold of that truth and plant it deep into our hearts? We can make every decision with the mind of Christ.

We can rest, because through the Holy Spirit, we have supernatural wisdom. We do not have to worry, fret, or fear because we have the revelations of the Spirit of God. Peace abides within us.

Having the mind of Christ means we have the power to exercise sound judgment. "*For God did not give us a spirit of timidity or cowardice or fear, but [He has given us a spirit] of power and of love and of sound judgment and personal discipline [abilities that result in a calm, well-balanced mind and self-control]"* (2 Timothy 1:7 AMP). When we exercise sound judgment, we are calm and emotionally or psychologically untroubled, i.e., of a well-balanced mind.

That sounds amazing, and maybe even too good to be true or idyllic. Well, it takes discipline. Jesus said, *"Peace I leave with you; My [perfect] peace I give to you; not as the world gives do I give to you. Do not let your heart be troubled, nor let it be afraid. [Let My perfect peace calm you in every circumstance and give you courage and strength for every challenge]"* (John 14:27 AMP). Notice the word "let." *Let* means "to allow, permit, or cause to." This implies that we have control over it. Do not allow your heart to be troubled. Do not cause your heart to be afraid. Permit HIS abiding rest, His perfect peace, to calm you in EVERY circumstance. Operating from a place of rest with the mind of Christ means being intentional about how we allow our mind to work.

Remember, it was only two chapters later that Jesus admonished, *"I have told you these things, so that in Me you may have [perfect] peace. In the world you have tribulation and distress and suffering, but be courageous [be confident, be undaunted, be filled with joy]; I have overcome the world." [My conquest is accomplished, My victory abiding]"* (John 16:33 AMP). Jesus confirms that the recipe for having the mind of Christ is abiding IN HIM. When we abide in Him, we can BE confident and undaunted. When there is chaos all around, we can resolve to remain at rest. If Jesus modeled peace in the storm—not just *speaking* peace to the storm, but *being* peace in the storm—we can do that, too.

Philippians 2:5 (TPT) says, *"And consider the example that Jesus, the Anointed One, has set before us. Let His mindset become your motivation.*" So, let's consider Jesus' example: He was sound asleep in the middle of a terrible storm. Likewise, we can call to mind God's faithfulness and choose not to allow the worries, the shoulda-coulda-wouldas, the what ifs, or the character and quality of the storm to rob us of rest. We can purpose to lean into the character of Christ and live from the thoughts, feelings, and purposes of God.

Proverbs providers further instruction in this regards: "*Fill your thoughts with my words until they penetrate deep into your spirit. Then, as you unwrap my words, they will impart true life and radiant health into the very core of your being.*" (Proverbs 4:21-22 TPT). The partnership that is available to us through the Covenant Peace, in one in which our participation includes disciplining our minds to think like Jesus. Paul repeats this instruction in his letter to the church at Colossae: "*Set your mind and keep focused habitually on the things above [the heavenly things], not on the things that are on the earth [which have only temporal value].*" (Colossians 3:2 AMP).

Let me try to explain the recipe differently. "*You will keep in perfect and constant peace the one whose mind is steadfast [that is, committed and focused on You—in both inclination and character], Because he trusts and takes refuge in You [with hope and confident expectation]*" (Isaiah 26:3 AMP). We can operate from rest when our minds are focused on the I AM. When we completely trust Him, we can have constant peace. It is not easy to do. It requires discipline and sensitivity to Holy Spirit, and often accountability from the Pauls and Barnabases of our lives, to recognize when we aren't living from rest so we can get back there.

Let's look at Philippians 4:6-8 (WNT) again:

*"Do not be over-anxious about anything, but by prayer and earnest pleading, together with thanksgiving, let your request be unreservedly made known in the presence of God. And then the peace of God, which transcends all our powers of thought, will be a **garrison** to guard your hearts and minds in union with Christ Jesus. Finally, believers, whatever is true, whatever is honorable and worthy of respect, whatever is right and confirmed by God's word, whatever is pure and wholesome, whatever is lovely and brings peace, whatever is admirable and of good repute; if there is any excellence, if there is anything worthy of praise, **think continually on these things [center your mind on them, and implant them in your heart].**"*

Have the discipline to govern your thoughts.

"Do not be" means decide that you aren't going to allow your thoughts or emotions to run away with themselves.

"Think continually" means be alert, always be mindful or purposeful regarding that upon which you allow yourself to dwell.

When we exercise such discipline, He promised to provide a sophisticated military installation, a guard over our hearts and minds to protect the peace.

LORD, I BELIEVE, HELP MY UNBELIEF

I was disappointed when I didn't get the judge position I thought I was aiming for. I wasn't disappointed because I didn't get the job necessarily. I was discouraged because I didn't understand what that four-month process was all about. I thought I heard from the Lord. I thought I had multiple confirmations that I was in the center of His will. When it didn't work out as I expected, I was confused. I began to doubt my ability to hear God. I questioned all of those revelations.

But I recognized that questioning voice. I remembered that chaos, lies, and confusion bear the fingerprints of the enemy. You see, that voice was the one who questioned Eve in the garden: "Are you sure you will die if you eat the fruit?" It was the one that questioned Jesus in the desert: "Why not command these stones to become bread?" The thing was, I recognized the voice, but I still struggled to exchange his lie for the truth.

I did not know why I went through that experience, and the question gave way to doubt. In that in between space, while I didn't know how to replace the lie with the truth, I did know how to call to mind God's faithfulness and His promise to provide daily bread and a lamp under my feet. I did know how to rebuke myself for being frustrated that I had a low-lit lamp under my feet and not a flashlight into the future. As I began to shift my focus from the unknown to the known, I was able to re-acquire the peace.

On December 6, I discovered that the governor had not selected me to be a judge. On December 11, the mayor called me to ask if I would consider becoming the city's judge. I laughed. I laughed because I was reminded that His ways are higher than ours. Had I not considered the initial judgeship, I would not have been in a position to accept the one that God had for me. The city judge position was not full-time. This meant that I could keep my job with its salary and ADD to it the additional income of the city judge. GOD IS MY SOURCE!

Not only would I not have considered the position had it not been for the four-month-long process of the gubernatorial appointment, the city wouldn't have considered me for the job had they not seen the article in the newspaper indicating the committee had recommend me for appointment. One of the biggest psychological hurdles in the original process was the salary. I did not know how God would provide for my family if I took that significant pay cut. Then, not only did God increase my income, out of the testimony of becoming a judge, I was invited to speak at several events.

Let me just confess to you that the struggle was real. I was in and out of peace multiple times in the same day. Some of the moments of restlessness lasted longer than they should have. But I realized I had a weakness I was unaware of. Confusion was a new trigger. I did not like the questions without reason. In the past, when I had allowed anxiousness and worry to cloud my mind, it was because of grief, illness, issues with my children, stress over job stuff, or disagreements with my husband. For the most part, I've identified some cues or triggers arising out of those circumstances so that I can quickly recalibrate to peace.

The Lord graciously used this new situation to reveal an additional area that needed the refiner's fire. I have learned to pray like David: search me, oh God, for any anxious thought in me and lead me back to Your peace (see Psalm 139:23-24). Well, God was answering my prayer. It was kind of a long answer. In my prayer times, I've often asked the Lord to send me a book or a letter in the mail because it would be much faster and less painful. This was a lesson I couldn't learn without being in the confusion.

We've talked about the process of peace and mind change. Revealing the areas of restlessness and angst is part of the process. Holy Spirit reveals to us the areas that still need change.

Something must first be recognized before it can be modified. This lifestyle of peace, of abiding in rest, is not just about the character of Christ. We have a role to play, as well. We have to do our part and He will do His part.

TWO PARTY PEACE PACT

He provides the peace keeping as we supply the desire and commitment.

Our part:

> *"Remember to stay alert and hold firmly to all that you believe. Be mighty and full of courage."* (1 Corinthians 16:13 TPT)

> *"Wait for and confidently expect the Lord; Be strong and let your heart take courage; Yes, wait for and confidently expect the Lord."* (Psalm 27:14 AMP)

Our part is basically expecting God to do His part.
God's part:

> *"Now may God, the fountain of hope, fill you to overflowing with uncontainable joy and perfect peace as you trust in him. And may the power of the Holy Spirit continually surround your life with his super-abundance until you radiate with hope!"* (Romans 15:13 TPT)

He provides the "overflowing... uncontainable joy and perfect peace" _AS_ we trust Him to do just that. When we start to doubt, waiver, or falter, we do as David did and *"encourage and strengthen [ourselves] in the Lord [our] God"* (1 Samuel 30:6 AMPC).

Jude gives us further instructions: *"But you, my delightfully* *loved friends, **constantly and progressively build yourselves up** on the foundation of your most holy faith **by** praying every moment in the Spirit. **Fasten your hearts** to the love of God and **receive** the mercy of our Lord Jesus Christ, who gives us eternal life"* (Jude 20-21 TPT). Encourage yourself by praying without ceasing. Again, we find language describing a process and a decision. This process is "progressively building ourselves up." The decision is to "fasten our hearts."

The result is abiding in rest. Paul described this best in his second letter to Timothy:

> *"The confidence of my calling enables me to overcome every difficulty without shame, for I have an intimate revelation of this God. And my faith in him **convinces me** that he is more than able to keep all that I've placed in his hands safe and secure until the fullness of his appearing."*
> (2 Timothy 1:12 TPT)

Imagine if you could echo the words of Paul and unequivocally declare your confidence in Christ because He has divinely revealed Himself to you in such a way that convinces you He is your Source. Imagine that you are convinced that you have the authority to walk in His peace and power.

ACTIVATION

Maybe you're still in the "Lord I believe/help my unbelief" dichotomy. Let us practice together the discipline of controlling our minds. To better prepare our hearts, listen to "Faithful Now" by Vertical Worship and "Story I'll Tell" by Naomi Raine.

Pray with me:

> *Lord, in the same way that I committed my life to You and accepted Your gift of salvation, I commit my thoughts and emotions to You and accept Your gift of peace. Help me to be disciplined to call to mind Your goodness and faithfulness in every circumstance. By Your Spirit, remind me to think only of the things that are honorable and worthy of respect, that which is right and confirmed by Your word, that are pure and wholesome, that are lovely and bring peace, that are admirable and of good repute. When I become distracted, convict me. Fill me anew with uncontainable joy and perfect peace. Empower me to constantly expect YOU. Reveal Yourself to me and teach me to know You more. AMEN.*

I.   What is one thought or mindset in conflict with Philippians 4:8 over which you need to exercise authority? (What lie do you struggle not to believe about yourself or your situation?)

_____

_____

_____

_____

_____

2. What kind of thing tends to provoke this thought? (What type of situation, interaction, or experience happens before you consider believing the lie?)

    _____

    _____

    _____

    _____

    _____

    _____

    _____

3. What trigger can you give to yourself to heighten your awareness in this type of situation so that you can be on guard? (Is there anything concise or unique about the lie or circumstance, a word that you think of, or color that you see that would be a clue or key you would be able to recognize as an indication that you're starting to believe the lie again?)

    _____

    _____

    _____

    _____

    _____

    _____

    _____

4. What can you call to mind, instead, upon which you can direct your mind to dwell that aligns with Philippians 4:8? (What is the truth of the character and nature of God, or what is the opposite of the lie that your trigger can cause you to think about instead?)

_____

_____

_____

_____

_____

_____

5. What commitment are you willing to make to yourself to begin to practice a new thought process?

_____

_____

_____

_____

_____

_____

6. Turn your thoughts into a prayer of consecration. Write it down for later reflection.

_____

_____

_____

_____

_____

_____

CHAPTER 12

KINGDOM AUTHORITY

W HEN JESUS WAS instructing His disciples, He reminded them over and over again that the kingdom of God is not a future destination but an available habitation when we *abide in Him*. And it wasn't just for the chosen few. Instead, Jesus instructed them how to share the good news with everyone:

> *"The kingdom is not discovered in one place or another, for God's kingdom realm is already expanding within some of you."* (Luke 17:21 TPT)

> *"And as you go, preach this message: 'Heaven's kingdom realm is accessible, close enough to touch.' You must continually bring healing to lepers and to those who are sick, and make it your habit to break off the demonic presence from people, and raise the dead back to life. Freely you have received the power of the kingdom, so freely release it to others."* (Matthew 10:7-8 TPT)

*"Heal the sick, and tell them all, 'God's kingdom has arrived
and is now within your reach!'"* (Luke 10:9 TPT)

The Holy Spirit provides us access to the kingdom realm.
Paul explained this in Romans 14:17 (TPT) when he wrote, *"For
the kingdom of God is not a matter of rules about food and drink,
but is in the realm of the Holy Spirit, filled with righteousness, peace,
and joy."* I believe Paul was communicating that the kingdom of
God is a lifestyle; it is an operating system.

Jesus made it clear that kingdom authority has been given
to us. Now this isn't some sorcery or wizardry. This is the power
that David recognized when facing Goliath. In 1 Samuel 17:45
(NLT), David replied to the Philistine, *"You come to me with
sword, spear, and javelin, but I come to you in the name of the Lord
of Heaven's Armies—the God of the armies of Israel, whom you have
defied."*

God sent the manifestation of this kingdom authority to
Joshua at Jericho in Joshua chapter 5.

*"And then this, while Joshua was there near Jericho: He
looked up and saw right in front of him a man standing,
holding his drawn sword. Joshua stepped up to him and
said, 'Whose side are you on—ours or our enemies'?' He
said, 'Neither. I'm commander of God's army. I've just
arrived.' Joshua fell, face to the ground, and worshiped. He
asked, 'What orders does my Master have for his servant?'"*
(Joshua 5:13-14 MSG)

The Amplified version contains this note: "Whether the
divine messenger was an angel or the pre-incarnate Christ is
not clear from the Hebrew text; however, the message of godly

assistance and pending victory was made clear to Joshua by the encounter."

The Lord brings this portion of Scripture to my mind often. He reminds me that the captain of the Lord's army is much more equipped to fight this battle or handle the situation than I am. I pray you also experience this supernatural assistance that only God provides. Can you imagine hearing, "I have just arrived!" from the commander of the Lord's army? When we are aligned with Christ, this is our authority.

Jesus Himself admonished the disciples concerning the power He had given them in Luke's gospel:

> "One day Jesus called together his twelve disciples and gave them power and authority to cast out all demons and to heal all diseases." (Luke 9:1 NLT)

> "Look, I have given you authority over all the power of the enemy, and you can walk among snakes and scorpions and crush them. Nothing will injure you." (Luke 10:19 NLT)

I want to take just another moment to reflect on Luke 10:19. This time, let's consider the Amplified version:

> "Listen carefully: I have given you authority [that you now possess] to tread on serpents and scorpions, and [the ability to exercise authority] over all the power of the enemy (Satan); and nothing will [in any way] harm you."

I love that this version highlights the phrases that you NOW possess, and the ability to exercise authority. If only you could hear the excitement in my voice as I reread this verse with emphasis and enthusiasm. My friends, not only have we been given all authority, we possess this authority RIGHT NOW. AND we have the ability to exercise this authority over _ALL_ the power of the enemy.

I think there are some things in my own life for which I have handed my power over to the enemy, I don't know about you, but rereading this verse is empowering me to take back my God-given authority and ability to exercise power over the enemy and not the other way around.

In case you were concerned that perhaps Luke misunderstood, Matthew got the same message. He wrote:

> *"I will give you the keys of the kingdom of heaven; and whatever you bind on earth shall have been bound in heaven, and whatever you loose on earth shall have been loosed in heaven."* (Matthew 16:19 NASB)

We have the keys to the kingdom. When we bind, it was already bound. When we loose, it was already loosed. This means the authority is not contingent, it was predestined and preordained for us who are co-heirs with Christ.

John conveyed a similar message:

> *"I tell you this timeless truth: The person who follows me in faith, believing in me, will do the same mighty miracles that I do—even greater miracles than these because I go to be with my Father! For I will do whatever you ask me to do when you ask me in my name. And that is how the Son will show what the Father is really like and bring glory to him. Ask me anything in my name, and I will do it for you!"* (John 14:12-14 TPT)

And Paul wanted us to be reminded of that authority when he wrote to the churches in Rome and Ephesus:

*"Yes, God raised Jesus to life! And since **God's Spirit of Resurrection lives in you**, he will also raise your dying body to life **by the same Spirit that breathes life into you!**"* (Romans 8:11 TPT)

*"I pray that you will **continually experience the immeasurable greatness of God's power made available to you through faith.** Then your lives will be an advertisement of this **immense power as it works through you!** This is the mighty power that was released when God raised Christ from the dead and exalted him to the place of highest honor and supreme authority in the heavenly realm! And now he is exalted as first above every ruler, authority, government, and realm of power in existence! He is gloriously enthroned over every name that is ever praised, not only in this age, but in the age that is coming! And he alone is the leader and source of everything needed in the church. God has put everything beneath the authority of Jesus Christ and has given him the highest rank above all others. And now we, his church, are his body on the earth and that which fills him who is being filled by it!"* (Ephesians 1:19-23 TPT)

AN EXPERIENCE WITH KINGDOM AUTHORITY

We had finished moving to Kansas by the middle of August 2020. Immediately, the children took to the farm. Giuliana was so excited to collect eggs and chase chickens. We hadn't lived there more than a couple weeks when I got a call from the school. It was about thirty minutes before school got out and Giuliana had gotten sick and thrown up and I needed to go get her. I just assumed that perhaps the lunch didn't agree with her and all would be well.

In 2020, the school was adhering to COVID protocols which dictated that I call the school when I arrive and they would bring her outside. I got to the school, called the phone number, and stood outside the door on the cement patio. Giuliana walked out with the nurse. In the time it took me to sign my name on the clipboard, she had laid down on the ground and began vomiting. Something seemed very wrong. She was burning up. The nurse helped me get her to the car and I called Joshua and told him that he would need to come to the school. He couldn't understand why I would need help picking up children from school; it's not a two-parent job. But he heard the urgency in my voice and came.

When he got there, Giuliana was writhing in pain and told him she needed a hospital. We hadn't lived there long enough to know where the nearest children's hospital was. With the help of Google Maps, we quickly learned that the nearest hospital was a small local hospital, but it was only a few blocks away.

By the time I got her there, she was very lethargic and didn't have the strength to stand. As I walked through the double doors of the hospital carrying her lifeless-looking body across my arms, the staff of the hospital immediately noticed us and called for help. They didn't even get us registered. They just got a wheelchair. I sat down still carrying her and they wheeled us back to room. Since it was 2020, the first thing they did was rule out COVID.

At that point, they were still going up the nose with a long swab, nearly touching the brain. When she didn't even flinch or wince, the nurse said, "She will need to be transported downtown. She's beyond our capabilities here." She did not have COVID.

Ultimately, she was admitted to the children's hospital downtown. They determined she had infectious colitis caused by Salmonella. It would have to run its course, they said. In the meantime, we would do what we could to combat the symptoms. The primary concern was dehydration; she couldn't even sip water without vomiting.

Ultimately, five IVs failed and they had to give her a midline catheter. (A midline is an IV that goes up the arm to the brachial vein.) They brought in a special team to insert the line under ultrasound.

They failed.

Until now, I was communicating with Joshua by phone and he was at home caring for the other two children. Now five days had passed and I was very weary. When that midline failed, I called my sister. Thank God for family. My sister took my other children and Joshua could join us at the hospital.

They brought in an anesthesiology professional to make a second attempt to insert the midline catheter.

Success!

It was as if we could physically see God partnering with the medical team. She improved before our eyes. While she was being hydrated through the catheter, she was also able to keep down sips of water, which progressed to juice, and then she progressed to soft/bland foods.

Finally, she was strong enough to go home, and after a brief continued recovery at home, she was strong enough to return to school.

We know God healed her.

The doctors warned us that only time would tell if this was the first onset of chronic colitis. We would just have to keep a close eye on her. We would need to return to the hospital if any of these symptoms returned.

Then, one day about three weeks after she was discharged from the hospital, she laid down on my bedroom floor, grabbing her belly, tossing back and forth, screaming in pain. We anointed her with oil and prayed for her. Through tears she told us she needed a doctor; it was happening again. I threw some clothes in a bag and Joshua carried her to the car. The sound of her panicked and painful crying was deafening.

> "ABIDING IN REST IS NOT THE ABSENCE OF RESTLESSNESS. IT IS THE ABILITY TO RECOGNIZE WHEN WE FOCUS ON CHAOS AND NOT THE CREATOR WHO HOVERS OVER IT."

I pulled out of the driveway and down the street.

When I stopped at the stop sign, this righteous indignation and holy gumption rose inside me. I began to rebuke and bind sickness, disease, and all symptoms. I was passionately declaring the promises of God: "By His stripes we ARE healed." "It is finished." "I know You healed her weeks ago and we claim that healing even now." "Inflammation be gone in Jesus' name. Pain be gone in Jesus' name. Symptoms of whatever this is, is not of You. I loose the fullness of the manifestation of complete healing in Jesus' name."

This was not a long prayer. It was maybe a minute while stopped at the stop sign. As I continued driving, I noticed that the crying had stopped. She was sound asleep.

We got about 20-25 minutes into a 40-minute drive. She woke up. She sat straight up, smiling with light in her eyes.

"Mommy, I'm hungry. I need some dinner."

I called my husband. He said, "Well, we prayed. We believed God would heal her. Let's confirm. Just take her to the nearest urgent care and let them check her out. If they clear her, come on home." We did just that. We went to the nearest urgent care. They looked her over and checked her vital signs. They listened to me telling of the history and why we came. They said I was right to bring her based on the history and the symptoms I described.

But then the doctor said, "She has none of those symptoms now, and nothing from my exam would lead me to believe that she needs medical treatment. I think you are okay to take her back home. If the symptoms reoccur, we are not capable of dealing with that here. You will need to take her straight to the children's hospital."

Giuliana said, "I won't need to go to the hospital. Jesus told me I was healed."

I called Joshua back and told him we were on our way home.

She has never had another symptom like that in the two and a half years since.

I share this story to illustrate the process. For our family, it was appropriate to take her to the hospital AND call down heaven. We deal with what is while we expect God to do the supernatural. Abiding in rest is not the absence of restlessness. It is the ability to recognize when we focus on chaos and not the Creator who hovers over it. Abiding is not an event. It's a development that occurs as we grow in intimacy with Christ.

ACTIVATION

Let's listen to "Authority" by Elevation Worship and "Echo (In Jesus' Name)" by Charity Gayle before we begin to answer the activation questions.

1. When you started reading this chapter, what one thing or area of your life came to your mind as something over which it is time to exercise kingdom authority?

    _____

    _____

    _____

    _____

    _____

    _____

2. What verse are you ready to adopt as your prayer of consecration as you partner with Holy Spirit and take back the authority you may have relinquished?

    _____

    _____

    _____

    _____

    _____

    _____

3. What trigger or signal can you give to yourself to remind yourself that you have all authority to bind and loose and trample scorpions? (For me, it's the word "can't." When I

hear myself thinking or saying the word "can't," I am reminded to pause and seek the Lord to see if this is an area where I have abandoned God-given authority.)

_____

_____

_____

_____

_____

_____

4. Invite Holy Spirit to partner with you in divine exchange as you identify the trigger or signal that may indicate a relinquishment of authority, to reveal to you what you can replace the word or phrase with to exercise authority.

_____

_____

_____

_____

_____

5. Write a short prayer of consecration sealing the promise God has given you about your kingdom authority.

_____

_____

_____

_____

_____

CONCLUSION

THANK YOU FOR exploring the *Gospel is Rest*. My prayer is that you are more equipped to work, parent, minster, and friend from a place of rest instead of toward a place of rest, that you are at least interested in kicking the tires of the idea of working from the weekend. I trust that Holy Spirit is working in you, transforming your thoughts and mindsets. I have invited Him, on your behalf, to turn up the volume of His promptings, to quicken you when you fall out of rest and revert to straining and striving. I trust that peace will become a new practice, and then a habit.

My prayer for you and hope for your continued life's journey is found in Ephesians 3:16-19 (AMP):

> *"May He grant you out of the riches of His glory, to be* ***strengthened and spiritually energized*** *with power through His Spirit in your inner self, [indwelling your innermost being and personality], so that Christ may dwell in your hearts through your faith. And may you, having*

been [deeply] rooted and [securely] grounded in love, be fully capable of comprehending with all the saints (God's people) the width and length and height and depth of His love [fully experiencing that amazing, endless love]; and [that you may come] to know [practically, through personal experience] the love of Christ which far surpasses [mere] knowledge [without experience], that you may be filled up [throughout your being] to all the fullness of God [so that you may have the richest experience of God's presence in your lives, completely filled and flooded with God Himself.]"

If nothing else, I hope that you have discovered some tools and strategies to:

1. Be strengthened and spiritually energized;
2. Be rooted and grounded in love;
3. Experience that amazing, endless love;
4. Be filled up to all the fullness of God, completely filled and flooded with God Himself.

I hope that I have enticed you to consider a new operating system. As you reflect on this new paradigm and take time to digest some of the principles to rest and live from rest, I pray that you allow Holy Spirit to recalibrate, reprogram your attitude, thought process, and behavior. At the very least, I anticipate that you have begun to believe that you are designed for rest and have identified some steps you can take to become still and more confident in the knowledge of Christ.

I invite you to revisit the pages and chapters of this book and re-engage with the activations to grow even more resolved to abide in Christ. Maybe you have already thought of ways to consecrate time in His presence, whether setting your alarm thirty minutes earlier, or putting lunch appointments on your calendar, or retiring to your bedroom at night ahead of your previous bedtime.

Perhaps you have recorded, on note cards, some of the verses we have explored and posted them about your house in conspicuous places to remind you of the promises you are claiming over yourself. I challenge you to engage in a couple of new practices of living from a position of rest. Conceivably, some of the ideas we've discussed initiated some ideas of your own.

I believe we have unlocked a new awareness to the kingdom realm which we have access to. I pray that awareness becomes heightened as these concepts are ruminating in your spirit.

Imagine if the people of God assumed their positions as the rightful co-heirs with Christ in their positions of civil responsibility and leadership. Envision the fears that once kept you from obtaining your full potential were taken captive. What if we each saw ourselves as soldiers in God's army and we all began to see ourselves as God intended? What if each of us encountered an increased intimacy as we abide in Christ, and we're empowered to walk in the fullness of that power which lives in us? What would it be like if all of God's people lived from a position of rest?

As a prayer of consecration, I invite you to worship to the song "Shepherd," by CeCe Winans.

ABOUT THE AUTHOR

JACKLYN PALETTA is a licensed attorney in Michigan, Missouri, and Kansas. She has been the recipient of many legal accolades in recognition for excellence and achievements by the legal community, including Super Lawyers Rising Star, Outstanding Young Women Lawyers, and *American Law Society's* America's Top Lawyers. She is an international speaker, life coach, and mentor. She lives with her husband and three children on their farm raising sheep, chickens, and ducks. Jacklyn believes God's sustaining grace is continuously revealed by the message given to Mary (and each of us) in Luke 1:28: "You are highly favored and the Lord is with you." *The Gospel IS Rest* is her second book.

ALSO BY JACKLYN PALETTA

From Fear to Freedom: *Fueled by Faith as I Escaped Abuse*

Published in 2022, Paletta's first book is a raw, yet compelling
memoir of her journey to freedom from domestic violence.

The title is available on Amazon.com.

ENDNOTES

1. Carnes, Cody. "Firm Foundation." Digital download. Sparrow, Capital Music Group, 2021.

2. Vol. 53 No. 1; www.apa.org/monitor/2022/01/special-burn-out-stress; accessed September 21, 2022

3. Everyonesocial.com/blog/employee-burnout-statistics/ accessed September 21, 2022

4. Hetland, Leif. Called to Reign. Convergence Press, 2017.

5. See Merriam-Webster.com

6. See International Children's Bible, Expanded Bible, Good News Translation, New Century Version.

7. https://forwhatsaiththescriptures.org/2016/08/19/lord-of-sabaoth/ ESCHATOLOGY (END TIMES) / PROPHECY, What does "Lord of Sabaoth" mean? 08/19/2016 Christian ambassador (Shawn Brasseaux) (accessed 10/9/2022)

8. https://collinsdictionary

9. Power. (2005, August 1). https://www.bibletools.org/index.cfm/fuseaction/Library.sr/CT/ARTB/k/1067/power.htm

Made in the USA
Las Vegas, NV
30 September 2023